Between Us

touchstones

Between Us

edited by

HENRY J. BARON
BRUCE HEKMAN
DANIEL VANDER ARK

The National Union of Christian Schools

William B. Eerdmans Publishing Company
Grand Rapids, Michigan

865 Twenty-eighth Street, S.E., Grand Rapids, MI 49508.

ISBN 0-8028-1534-0.

Printed in the United States of America.

HENRY J. BARON received his B.A. from Calvin College, his M.A. from the University of Michigan, and his Ph.D. from the University of Illinois.

Dr. Baron taught in grades 5-12 at Sumas Christian School, Sumas, Washington, and South Christian High School, Grand Rapids, Michigan. He has taught classes at Grand Rapids Junior College, Grand Valley State College, and the University of Illinois and is presently Assistant Professor of English at Calvin College.

Author and editor of several articles, monographs, and curriculum guides, Dr. Baron is director of the *TOUCHSTONES* project and Language Arts Consultant for the National Union of Christian Schools.

BRUCE HEKMAN received his B.A. from Calvin College, his M.A. from the University of Michigan, and his Ph.D. from the University of Illinois.

Dr. Hekman taught at South Christian High School in Grand Rapids, Michigan. He is presently teaching and chairing the English Department at Chicago Christian High School, Palos Heights, Illinois.

Author of several articles and NUCS curriculum publications, Dr. Hekman has also conducted workshops and research in English programs for NUCS secondary schools.

DANIEL VANDER ARK earned his B.A. from Calvin College and his M.A. from the University of Nebraska.

Mr. Vander Ark teaches at Holland Christian High School, where he is chairman of the English Department. He is an author of four of the NUCS nine-week units in high school language arts: *Man and the Outcast, Man and the Search for Self, Man and the Search for Spiritual Significance,* and *Language and Man.*

Editorial services and design were provided by Sandra L. Vander Zicht, NUCS Curriculum Editor, and by Jon Pott, Marlin Van Elderen, Milton Essenburg, and Joel Beversluis of the Wm. B. Eerdmans Publishing Company.

The work presented herein was developed by the NUCS Curriculum Department, supported by a grant from the Christian School Educational Foundation.

CONTENTS

Together

PREFACE

TOUCHSTONES began as a revision of *THE PILOT SERIES IN LITERATURE, Book Three,* published by the NUCS in 1964. *TOUCHSTONES'* editors wrote a teacher's guide for *Book Three* in 1970, entitled *Thematic Literature Units 9,* in which they suggested many new selections and a new organizational pattern. This pattern developed the four themes now used in the *TOUCHSTONES* series: "Around Us," "Within Us," "Between Us," and "Above Us." *TOUCHSTONES* incorporates additional new selections, a modified version of the thematic organization, and new photos in a convenient and flexible format.

Underlying this new text is the conviction that curriculum materials should exhibit as equally as possible three major dimensions of Christian education—intellectual, decisional, and creative. We trust that the literature in *TOUCHSTONES* will promote personal growth along these lines. Through the thematic and generic focus in each book, the student can grow intellectually by learning about universal human experiences and concerns and about the artist's craft. As he is caught up in the tensions and conflicts of literature, he can grow in the attitudes and values that so strongly influence basic decisions in life. And he can grow creatively by responding to the literature in his own speaking, writing, and acting.

HENRY J. TRIEZENBERG, Ph.D.
NUCS Curriculum Administrator

DONALD OPPEWAL, Ph.D.
NUCS Policy Consultant

PHOTO CREDITS

Dave Pott, p. 3
H. Armstrong Roberts, pp. 32, 241
Steven Friedman, pp. 73, 96, 245
Paul M. Schrock, p. 86
John Arms, pp. 150-151
David Hoekema, p. 158

ILLUSTRATIONS

An original drawing by Armand Merizon, p. 161

ACKNOWLEDGMENTS

"The Quarrel." Copyright 1933, Renewal, © 1961 by Eleanor Farjeon. From the book *Poems for Children* by Eleanor Farjeon. Copyright 1951 by Eleanor Farjeon. Reprinted by permission of J. B. Lippincott Company; and Harold Ober Associates Incorporated.

"Come Go with Me" by B. T. Holm. © 1971 Scholastic Magazines, Inc. Reprinted by permission of Scholastic Magazines, Inc.

"Cain and Abel" (Genesis 4:1-16), from the Revised Standard Version Bible. Reprinted by permission of the National Council of the Churches of Christ in the U.S.A.

"Two Soldiers." Copyright 1942, renewed 1970 by Estelle Faulkner and Jill Faulkner. From *Collected Stories of William Faulkner* by William Faulkner. Reprinted by permission of Random House, Inc.

"I Got a Name" by Zachary Gold. Reprinted by permission of Mrs. Alma Hollins.

"Husbands and Wives" by Miriam Hershenson, copyright 1934 by Scholastic Magazines, Inc. Reprinted by permission of Scholastic Magazines, Inc.

"The Undercurrent." Copyright 1956 (In Renewal) By Fay Ehlert. Copyright 1928 by The Drama Magazine. First Revision copyright 1929 by Fay Ehlert. International copyright 1929 by Fay Ehlert. Reprinted by permission of Samuel French, Inc.

"The Whipping" by Robert Hayden. From *Selected Poems.* Copyright © 1966 by Robert Hayden. Reprinted by permission of October House Inc.

"My Papa's Waltz." Copyright 1942 by Hearst Magazines, Inc. From the book *Collected Poems of Theodore Roethke.* Reprinted by permission of Doubleday and Company, Inc.

"Hannah Armstrong," from *Spoon River Anthology* by Edgar

Lee Masters. Published by The Macmillan Company. Used by permission of Ellen C. (Mrs. Edgar Lee) Masters.

"Pick of the Season" by Warren J. Halliburton. Used by permission of the author.

"The Bench" by Richard Rive. Taken from *An African Treasury* edited by Langston Hughes. © 1960 by Langston Hughes. Used by permission of Crown Publishers, Inc.

"After You, My Dear Alphonse." Copyright 1943, 1949 by Shirley Jackson, copyright renewed 1971 by Laurence Hyman, Barry Hyman, Mrs. Sarah Webster, Mrs. Joanne Schnurer. From *The Lottery* by Shirley Jackson. Reprinted by permission of Farrar, Straus & Giroux, Inc.

"Three Who Went Looking for Death." Adapted by Elizabeth Wice from Chaucer's "Pardoner's Tale." © 1970 by Scholastic Magazines, Inc. Reprinted by permission of Scholastic Magazines, Inc.

"The Two Climbers" by Glenn Meeter. From *Being '71: An Anthology of Writing from "For the Time Being,"* compiled by Cor W. Barendrecht. Copyright 1971 by Workgroup Christian Writers, Box 1269, Grand Rapids, MI 49501. Reprinted by permission.

"The Man He Killed" by Thomas Hardy. From *Collected Poems* by Thomas Hardy. Copyright 1926 by The Macmillan Company. Reprinted by permission of The Macmillan Company; the Trustees of the Hardy Estate; Macmillan London & Basingstoke; and The Macmillan Company of Canada Limited.

"The Sniper," from *Spring Sowing* by Liam O'Flaherty. Reprinted by permission of Harcourt Brace Jovanovich, Inc. Also from *The Short Stories of Liam O'Flaherty*, reprinted by permission of Jonathan Cape Ltd., London.

"Hate" by James Stephens. From *Collected Poems of James Stephens.* Copyright 1909 by The Macmillan Company. Reprinted by permission of The Macmillan Company; and The Society of Authors as the literary representative of the Estate of James Stephens.

"The Last Flower." Copyright © 1939, 1961 by James Thurber. Published by Harper & Row. Used by permission of Mrs. James Thurber.

"Choose," from *Chicago Poems* by Carl Sandburg. Copyright, 1916, by Holt, Rinehart and Winston, Inc.; copyright, 1944, by Carl Sandburg. Reprinted by permission of Harcourt Brace Jovanovich, Inc.

"They Watched Her Die," from the book *Thirty-eight Witnesses* by A. M. Rosenthal. Copyright © 1964 by The New York Times. Used with permission of McGraw-Hill Book Company.

"A Helping Hand" by Miroslav Holub, trans. George Theiner. From *Miroslav Holub: Selected Poems*, translated by Ian Milner and George Theiner. Copyright © Miroslav Holub, 1967. Translations copyright © Ian Milner and George Theiner, 1967. Reprinted by permission of Penguin Books Ltd.

"Loneliness" by Brooks Jenkins. Copyright 1935 by Scholastic Magazines, Inc. Reprinted by permission of Scholastic Magazines, Inc.

"A Time to Talk," from *The Poetry of Robert Frost* edited by Edward Connery Lathem. Copyright 1916, © 1969 by Holt, Rinehart and Winston, Inc. Copyright 1944 by Robert Frost. Reprinted by permission of Holt, Rinehart and Winston, Inc.

"Split Cherry Tree" by Jesse Stuart. Reprinted by permission of *Esquire Magazine*. © 1938 (renewed 1966) by Esquire, Inc.

"Thank You, M'am." Copyright 1959 by Langston Hughes. Reprinted by permission of Harold Ober Associates Incorporated.

"We Are But a Moment's Sunlight," from "Let's Get Together" by Chet Powers. Copyright 1965, Irving Music, Inc. (BMI) All Rights Reserved. Used by permission.

"David and Jonathan" (1 Samuel 18, 19, 20), from the Revised Standard Version Bible. Reprinted by permission of the National Council of the Churches of Christ in the U.S.A.

"The Oyster and the Pearl" by William Saroyan. Used by permission of the author.

"Ha'Penny." Reprinted from *Tales from a Troubled Land* by Alan Paton by permission of Charles Scribner's Sons. Copyright © 1961 Alan Paton.

"The Gift of the Magi," from *The Four Million* by O. Henry. Reprinted by permission of Doubleday & Company, Inc.

"This Thing Called Love Is Pathological" by Lawrence Casler. Reprinted from *Psychology Today* magazine, December 1969. Copyright © Communications/Research/Magazines, Inc.

"The Practice of Love" (our title). Abridged from pp. 123-124, 126-129 in *The Art of Loving* by Erich Fromm. Copyright ©

1956 by Erich Fromm. By permission of Harper & Row, Publishers, Inc.

"The Greatest of These Is Love" (1 Corinthians 13) and "All Are Needed by Each One" (1 Corinthians 12), from *The Living Bible.* Reprinted by permission of Tyndale House Publishers.

"The Prodigal Son," from *God's Trombones* by James Weldon Johnson. Copyright 1927 by The Viking Press, Inc., renewed 1955 by Grace Nail Johnson. All rights reserved. Reprinted by permission of The Viking Press, Inc.

"The Revolutionary" and "Perfect Love Banishes Fear." Reprinted from *Listen to the Green* by Luci Shaw, © 1971 by Harold Shaw Publishers, Box 567, Wheaton, IL 60187. Used by permission.

"Through the Midst of the Sea on Dry Ground" by E. William Oldenburg. From *Being '71: An Anthology of Writing from "For the Time Being,"* compiled by Cor W. Barendrecht. Copyright 1971 by Workgroup Christian Writers, Box 1269, Grand Rapids, MI 49501. Used by permission.

"Passion for Compassion" and "Safe at Sea," from *You! Jonah!* by Thomas John Carlisle. Published by Wm. B. Eerdmans Publishing Company.

TO THE STUDENT

"No man is an island," said a poet long ago. Still, people do sometimes feel like islands, cut off from the land, alone on an unfriendly ocean.

For things can go wrong between people. Misunderstandings and prejudices can separate them. Angry words can kill a relationship. Husbands and wives quit speaking. Brothers and sisters quit caring about each other. Friends become enemies.

But when all has been said and done, and the heat of passion begins to cool, the awful feeling of loneliness and separateness sets in. Maybe you've experienced it. Not many of us escape breakdowns of communication, feelings of irritation and contempt, and words of hostility and bitterness.

Our basic need is for togetherness. A place of belonging. Persons with whom we can share our time, our thoughts, our love.

This book is about relationships—relationships between people. You will read about some that are fragile and break, and about others that are nurtured into strong and beautiful structures.

Most of all, the stories, plays, and poems in this book are about you—about all of us who are still learning the hard lesson: to love our neighbor as ourselves.

HENRY J. BARON
Project Director

Differences

The Quarrel

I quarreled with my brother,
I don't know what about,
One thing led to another
And somehow we fell out.
The start of it was slight,
The end of it was strong,
He said he was right,
I knew he was wrong!

We hated one another.
The afternoon turned black.
Then suddenly my brother
Thumped me on the back,
And said, "Oh, come along!
We can't go on all night—
I was in the wrong."
So he was in the right.

Eleanor Farjeon

You have a paradox when two things that seem to be opposites are found together. Can you identify and explain the paradox in this poem?

Come Go with Me

B. T. Holm

Finally the bell rang and typing class and school were over for the day. Sandy quickly pulled the cover over her typewriter and left her speed test on Mrs. Ford's desk.

"Hey, wait for me, Sandy." She turned and saw Gail smiling at her.

"Hi, Gail. How'd you do on the test?"

"Terrible." They walked slowly through the crowded halls to the locker room. "I get so nervous I can't even type my name right. And I left out two whole sentences. How can I be a secretary if I can only type ten words a minute with ten errors?"

Sandy laughed. "I got my name right today, but I kept typing *the* backwards. And you know something—every time we're supposed to take a speed test I just break up. All those typewriters going together sound like a hundred people tapdancing like mad. Mrs. Ford must think I'm crazy, sitting there with a dumb smile on my face."

"Sit next to me tomorrow. We'll type notes instead of those stupid business letters." Gail was at her locker. As Sandy went on to her own, Gail said, "Why don't you come and have a Coke with us? We're going down to Lucy's for a while."

"Maybe some other time. I'm meeting Lorraine today."

"Well, okay." Gail combed her hair and grabbed her books. "I've gotta run. See you tomorrow. Be sure to save me a seat in typing."

Gail had gone. Sandy jerked open her locker. There was a candy bar on the shelf with a note from Lorraine: Live it up. Only 43 more typing classes to go.

She stuck the candy bar in her pocket, dumped most of her books, and went out to meet Lorraine. Even in the crowd around the front door it wasn't hard to find her. She was the only girl in school who wore her hair in a long braid down her back. And she was very big. Sandy was glad to see her. "Hi. Thanks for the candy bar."

"Don't think it wasn't a sacrifice. It was really for me, but Miss Ryan took me off the volleyball court to give me a big lecture about losing weight. So I felt very guilty about eating it myself. But maybe we could split it."

"You pig! You'll never lose weight. Here."

Sandy split the candy bar and they started walking down Colfax Avenue. "You'll never believe what Margo did in sewing class today," Lorraine said. "It was great."

"What'd she do? Better than last time?"

"Well, while Miss Jones was talking about zippers Margo cut up the tape measures and threw them out the window. Then she pulled out one of her boy friend's cigars and lit it. I thought Miss Jones would faint."

"What happened?"

"Miss Jones said, 'Margo, it's only because of Mr. Daley's kindness that you're even in this school.' And Margo said, 'The same goes for you.' Then Miss Jones kicked Margo out of class and we went on with the zippers."

"I wish good stuff like that would happen in my sewing class. It's just a big bore. Nobody ever does anything," said Sandy. "I wish you were in my class. We'd have fun. It might even help get my ugly skirt finished."

They crossed the street and came up to Lucy's, which was filled with high school students. Lorraine called it The Zoo and said it was worse than the school cafeteria.

Sandy had been in a few times and had really liked it. There was something about being in the right place with people the rest of the school looked up to. But this time she walked past, trying to look cool and casual.

"Do you wanna stop in?" Lorraine asked suddenly. "I've got some money. I don't mind."

Sandy was startled. "Oh, no, not today. It's so crowded in there. You can't even hear yourself think. Who needs it?"

"Okay. Whatever you say." Then Lorraine began to hum the background of their favorite old song, "Come Go with Me." Sandy picked it up and the two of them walked along, singing seriously, unaware of anything else.

Suddenly the spell was broken. "Hey Lorraine, watch where you're going!"

They stood dumbly in front of the supermarket, looking at Linda Larson's groceries on the ground.

"Oh, I'm sorry, Linda," Lorraine mumbled. She bent awkwardly to pick up the bag. Linda tossed back her hair and looked at Sandy. "I didn't know you could sing, Sandy."

"Oh, we just kid around. It's Lorraine who can really—"

"Well, I've got to be going," Linda interrupted. She took the bag of groceries. "Listen, Sandy, are you going to be home tonight? There's something I'd like to talk to you about. I'll call you about nine. Okay?" Before Sandy could say anything, Linda turned and walked quickly to her boyfriend's car. She waved good-bye as he pulled into traffic.

They were almost at Lorraine's corner. "Gee, how does it feel to be noticed by the lovely Linda Larson?" she said. "I didn't think she talked to us ordinary folks."

"Don't be sarcastic. She probably just wants the history homework or something."

"Yeah. Or something. Well, I've gotta go. Why don't you come over? You haven't seen the new kittens yet."

"No—I'd better not. I told my mother I'd clean my room. I'll see you tomorrow."

"Okay. Have a nice talk with Linda. Give her my love."

They parted and Sandy walked the rest of the way slowly, feeling something funny in her stomach. It wasn't every day that Linda Larson called up.

At 8:30 she started to bite her nails. She lay on the bed and wrote in her notebook in different kinds of handwriting: Sandy and Douglas Banner. Douglas Banner was part of Linda and Gail's crowd. Both he and Sandy had trouble with algebra and once they had worked on it together. Last month he had thrown a spitball at her. She would never forget the smile on his face. She was scared sick of him. "I love Douglas Banner," Sandy said softly. What would Lorraine say?

She jumped when the phone rang. "I'll get it!" she shouted. She sat down in the hall. "Hello?"

"Sandy, it's me—Linda."

"Oh, hi, Linda," she said casually. Then she yelled, "Bobby, get out of here! That darn brother of mine. He's always snooping around."

"I know what you mean. My brother's a brat, too. But I think I'm getting my own phone for my birthday. A white one."

"Gee, that's great."

They talked for a while about school, about clothes, about boys. Sandy picked nervously at a chip of paint. She hasn't asked me for the homework yet. What does she want?

Finally, Linda said, "Well, I really called to see if

you'd like to come over to my house tomorrow night. We're going to play records and just fool around."

"Oh, I'd really like to, Linda. That would be fun. I'd love to. Do you think I could bring Lorraine, too?"

There was a pause. "Well—no. I mean, Lorraine just doesn't fit in with us. She's strange, you know, the way she looks and dresses and all. In fact, none of us can figure out why you stick with her. It's not like we're back in grade school, you know."

"I know. Lorraine isn't really what you think. If you knew her, you'd see that she—"

"All I know is that she's keeping you back. We'd love to have you in our crowd, Sandy. But you can't bring her with you. We just can't have her."

"But Lorraine is my friend. I couldn't hurt her like that."

"Well, I don't mean to be cruel. I know she means a lot to you and all that. But be realistic. Even Douglas Banner was asking about you. I think he really likes you."

"Ha! Douglas Banner. What does he know. He can't even do algebra."

"Well, you just think about it. It's not really so hard. You remember me and Betty Roberts back in sixth grade. It was almost the same thing. Just because you live near somebody is no reason to hang around with her all the time."

"With Lorraine it's really not that. She's a wonderful—"

"Let's not fight about it, Sandy. Just meet me and Gail after school tomorrow. You'll see we're right."

"Well, maybe I could," said Sandy softly.

"Great. I'll meet you at Gail's locker, and we'll go to Lucy's. I'll see you then. Bye-bye."

"Good-bye." Sandy hung up the phone and went

back to her room. Her hands were wet and she felt sad in her throat. She lay down on the bed and stared at the ceiling.

I dread tomorrow, she thought. I don't want it to come. I wish I was only two years old, then I wouldn't have to feel this way. What can I tell Lorraine? What am I going to do?

What *did* Sandy do? What would *you* have done in similar circumstances?

Cain and Abel

(Genesis 4:1-16)

[1]Now Adam knew Eve his wife, and she conceived
and bore Cain, saying, "I have gotten a man with the
help of the LORD." [2]And again, she bore his brother
Abel. Now Abel was a keeper of sheep, and Cain a tiller
of the ground. [3]In the course of time Cain brought to
the LORD an offering of the fruit of the ground, [4]and
Abel brought of the firstlings of his flock and of their
fat portions. And the LORD had regard for Abel and his
offering, [5]but for Cain and his offering he had no
regard. So Cain was very angry, and his countenance
fell. [6]The LORD said to Cain, "Why are you angry, and
why has your countenance fallen? [7]If you do well, will
you not be accepted? And if you do not do well, sin is
couching at the door; its desire is for you, but you must
master it."

[8]Cain said to Abel his brother, "Let us go out to the field." And when they were in the field, Cain rose up against his brother Abel, and killed him. [9]Then the LORD said to Cain, "Where is Abel your brother?" He said, "I do not know; am I my brother's keeper?" [10] And the LORD said, "What have you done? The voice of your brother's blood is crying to me from the ground. [11] And now you are cursed from the ground, which has opened its mouth to receive your brother's blood from your hand. [12]When you till the ground, it shall no longer yield to you its strength; you shall be a fugitive and a wanderer on the earth." [13]Cain said to the LORD, "My punishment is greater than I can bear. [14]Behold, thou hast driven me this day away from the ground; and from thy face I shall be hidden; and I shall be a fugitive and a wanderer on the earth, and whoever finds me will slay me." [15]Then the LORD said to him, "Not so! If any one slays Cain, vengeance shall be taken on him sevenfold." And the LORD put a mark on Cain, lest any who came upon him should kill him. [16]Then Cain went away from the presence of the LORD, and dwelt in the land of Nod, east of Eden.

The Revised Standard Version

Who is your brother?

Where is your brother?

Two Soldiers

William Faulkner

Me and Pete would go down to Old Man Killegrew's and listen to his radio. We would wait until after supper, after dark, and we would stand outside Old Man Killegrew's parlor window, and we could hear it because Old Man Killegrew's wife was deaf, and so he run the radio as loud as it would run, and so me and Pete could hear it plain as Old Man Killegrew's wife could, I reckon, even standing outside with the window closed.

And that night I said, "What? Japanese? What's a pearl harbor?" and Pete said, "Hush."

And so we stood there, it was cold, listening to the fellow in the radio talking, only I couldn't make no heads nor tails neither out of it. Then the fellow said that would be all for a while, and me and Pete walked back up the road to home, and Pete told me what it was. Because he was nigh twenty and he had done finished the Consolidated last June and he knowed a heap: about them Japanese dropping bombs on Pearl Harbor and that Pearl Harbor was across the water.

"Across what water?" I said. "Across that Government reservoy up at Oxford?"

"Naw," Pete said. "Across the big water. The Pacific Ocean."

We went home. Maw and pap was already asleep, and me and Pete laid in the bed, and I still couldn't understand where it was, and Pete told me again—the Pacific Ocean.

"What's the matter with you?" Pete said. "You're going on nine years old. You been in school now ever since September. Ain't you learned nothing yet?"

"I reckon we ain't got as fer as the Pacific Ocean yet," I said.

We was still sowing the vetch then that ought to been all finished by the fifteenth of November, because pap was still behind, just like he had been ever since me and Pete had knowed him. And we had firewood to git in, too, but every night me and Pete would go down to Old Man Killegrew's and stand outside his parlor window in the cold and listen to his radio; then we would come back home and lay in the bed and Pete would tell me what it was. That is, he would tell me for a while. Then he wouldn't tell me. It was like he didn't want to talk about it no more. He would tell me to shut up because he wanted to go to sleep, but he never wanted to go to sleep.

He would lay there, a heap stiller than if he was asleep, and it would be something, I could feel it coming out of him, like he was mad at me even, only I knowed he wasn't thinking about me, or like he was worried about something, and it wasn't that neither, because he never had nothing to worry about. He never got behind like pap, let alone stayed behind. Pap give him ten acres when he graduated from the Consolidated, and me and Pete both reckoned pap was durn glad to get shut of at least ten acres, less to have to worry with himself; and Pete had them ten acres all sowed to vetch and busted out and bedded for the winter, and so it wasn't that. But it was something. And still we would go down to Old Man Killegrew's every night and listen to his radio, and they was at it in the Philippines now, but General MacArthur was holding um. Then we would come back home and lay in the bed, and Pete wouldn't tell me nothing or talk at all. He would just lay there still as an ambush and when I would touch him, his side or his leg would feel hard and still as iron, until after a while I would go to sleep.

Then one night—it was the first time he had said nothing to me except to jump on me about not chopping enough wood at the wood tree where we was cutting–he said, "I got to go."

"Go where?" I said.

"To that war," Pete said.

"Before we even finish gettin' in the firewood?"

"Firewood, heck," Pete said.

"All right," I said. "When we going to start?"

But he wasn't even listening. He laid there, hard and still as iron in the dark. "I got to go," he said. "I jest ain't going to put up with no folks treating the Unity States that way."

"Yes," I said. "Firewood or no firewood, I reckon we got to go."

This time he heard me. He laid still again, but it was a different kind of still.

"You?" he said. "To a war?"

"You'll whup the big uns and I'll whup the little uns," I said.

Then he told me I couldn't go. At first I thought he just never wanted me tagging after him, like he wouldn't leave me go with him when he went sparking them girls of Tull's. Then he told me the Army wouldn't leave me go because I was too little, and then I knowed he really meant it and that I couldn't go nohow noways. And somehow I hadn't believed until then that he was going himself, but now I knowed he was and that he wasn't going to leave me go with him a-tall.

"I'll chop the wood and tote the water for you-all then!" I said. "You got to have wood and water!"

Anyway, he was listening to me now. He wasn't like iron now.

He turned onto his side and put his hand on my chest because it was me that was laying straight and hard on my back now.

"No," he said. "You got to stay here and help pap."

"Help him what?" I said. "He ain't never caught up nohow. He can't get no further behind. He can sholy take care of this little shirttail of a farm while me and you are whupping them Japanese. I got to go too. If you got to go, then so have I."

"No," Pete said. "Hush now. Hush." And he meant it, and I knowed he did. Only I made sho from his own mouth. I quit.

"So I just can't go then," I said.

"No," Pete said. "You just can't go. You're too little, in the first place, and in the second place ——"

"All right," I said. "Then shut up and leave me go to sleep."

So he hushed then and laid back. And I laid there like I was already asleep, and pretty soon he was asleep and I knowed it was the wanting to go to the war that had worried him and kept him awake, and now that he had decided to go, he wasn't worried any more.

The next morning he told maw and pap. Maw was all right. She cried.

"No," she said, crying, "I don't want him to go. I would rather go myself in his place, if I could. I don't want to save the country. Them Japanese could take it and keep it, so long as they left me and my family and my children alone. But I remember my brother Marsh in that other war. He had to go to that one when he wasn't but nineteen, and our mother couldn't understand it then any more than I can now. But she told Marsh if he had to go, he had to go. And so, if Pete's got to go to this one, he's got to go to it. Jest don't ask me to understand why."

But pap was the one. He was the feller. "To the war?" he said. "Why, I just don't see a bit of use in that. You ain't old enough for the draft, and the country ain't being invaded. Our President in Washington, D.C., is watching the conditions and he will notify us. Besides, in that other war your ma just mentioned, I was drafted and sent clean to Texas and was held there nigh eight months until they finally quit fighting. It seems to me that that, along with your Uncle Marsh who received a actual wound on the battlefields of France, is enough for me and mine to have to do to protect the country, at least in my lifetime. Besides, what'll I do for help on the farm with you gone? It seems to me I'll get mighty far behind."

"You been behind as long as I can remember," Pete said. "Anyway, I'm going. I got to."

"Of course he's got to go," I said. "Them Japanese ——"

"You hush your mouth!" maw said, crying. "Nobody's talking to you! Go and get me a armful of wood! That's what you can do!"

So I got the wood. And all the next day, while me and Pete and pap was getting in as much wood as we could in that time because Pete said how pap's idea of plenty of wood was one more stick laying against the wall that maw ain't put on the fire yet, maw was getting Pete ready to go. She washed and mended his clothes and cooked him a shoe box of vittles. And that night me and Pete laid in the bed and listened to her packing his grip and crying, until after a while Pete got up in his nightshirt and went back there, and I could hear them talking, until at last maw said, "You got to go, and so I want you to go. But I don't understand it, and I won't never, and so don't expect me to." And Pete come back and got into the bed again and laid again still and hard as iron on his back, and then he said, and he wasn't talking to me, he wasn't talking to nobody: "I got to go. I just got to."

"Sho you got to," I said. "Them Japanese——" He

turned over hard, he kind of surged over onto his side, looking at me in the dark.

"Anyway, you're all right," he said. "I expected to have more trouble with you than with all the rest of them put together."

"I reckon I can't help it neither," I said. "But maybe it will run a few years longer and I can get there. Maybe someday I will jest walk in on you."

"I hope not," Pete said. "Folks don't go to wars for fun. A man don't leave his maw crying just for fun."

"Then why are you going?" I said.

"I got to," he said. "I just got to. Now you go on to sleep. I got to ketch that early bus in the morning."

"All right," I said, "I hear tell Memphis is a big place. How will you find where the Army's at?"

"I'll ask somebody where to go to join it," Pete said. "Go on to sleep now."

"Is that what you'll ask for? Where to join the Army?" I said.

"Yes," Pete said. He turned onto his back again. "Shut up and go to sleep."

We went to sleep. The next morning we et breakfast by lamplight because the bus would pass at six o'clock. Maw wasn't crying now. She jest looked grim and busy, putting breakfast on the table while we et it. Then she finished packing Pete's grip, except he never wanted to take no grip to the war, but maw said decent folks never went nowhere, not even to a war, without a change of clothes and something to tote them in. She put in the shoe box of fried chicken and biscuits and she put the Bible in, too, and then it was time to go. We didn't know until then that maw wasn't going to the bus. She jest brought Pete's cap and overcoat, and still she didn't cry no more, she jest stood with her hands on Pete's shoulders and she didn't move, but somehow, and just holding Pete's shoulders, she looked as hard and fierce as when Pete had turned toward me in the bed last night and tole me that anyway I was all right.

"They could take the country and keep the country, so long as they never bothered me and mine," she said. Then she said, "Don't never forget who you are. You ain't rich and the rest of the world outside of Frenchman's Bend never heard of you. But your blood is good as any blood anywhere, and don't you never forget it."

Then she kissed him, and then we was out of the house, with pap toting Pete's grip whether Pete wanted him to or not. There wasn't no dawn even yet, not even after we had stood on the highway by the mailbox, a while. Then we seen the lights of the bus coming and I was watching the bus until it come up and Pete flagged it, and then, sho enough, there was daylight–it had started while I wasn't watching. And now me and Pete expected pap to say something else foolish, like he done before, about how Uncle Marsh getting wounded in France and that trip to Texas pap had taken in 1918 ought to be enough to save the Unity States in 1942, but he never. He done all right too. He jest said, "Good-by, son. Always remember what your ma told you and write her whenever you find the time." Then he shaken Pete's hand, and Pete looked at me a minute and put his hand on my head and rubbed my head durn nigh hard enough to wring my neck off and jumped into the bus, and the feller wound the door shut and the bus began to hum; then it was moving, humming and grinding and whining louder and louder; it was going fast, with two little red lights behind it that never seemed to get no littler, but just seemed to be running together until pretty soon they would touch and jest be one light. But they never did, and then the bus was gone, and even like it was, I could have pretty nigh busted out crying, nigh to nine years old and all.

Me and pap went back to the house. All that day we

worked at the wood tree, and so I never had no good chance until about middle of the afternoon. Then I taken my slingshot and I would have liked to took all my bird eggs, too, because Pete had give me his collection and he holp me with mine, and he would like to git the box out and look at them as good as I would, even if he was nigh twenty years old. But the box was too big to tote a long ways and have to worry with, so I just taken the shikepoke egg, because it was the best un, and wropped it up good into a matchbox and hid it and the slingshot under the corner of the barn. Then we et supper and went to bed, and I thought then how if I would 'a' had to stayed in that room and that bed like that even for one more night, I jest couldn't 'a' stood it. Then I could hear pap snoring, but I never heard no sound from maw, whether she was asleep or not, and I don't reckon she was. So I taken my shoes and drapped them out the window, and then I clumb out like I used to watch Pete do when he was still jest seventeen and pap held that he was too young yet to be tomcatting around at night, and wouldn't leave him out, and I put on my shoes and went to the barn and got the slingshot and the shikepoke egg and went to the highway.

It wasn't cold, it was jest durn confounded dark, and that highway stretched on in front of me like, without nobody using it, it had stretched out half again as fer just like a man does when he lays down, so that for a time it looked like full sun was going to ketch me before I had finished them twenty-two miles to Jefferson. But it didn't. Daybreak was jest starting when I walked up the hill into town. I could smell breakfast cooking in the cabins and I wished I had thought to brought me a cold biscuit, but that was too late now. And Pete had told me Memphis was a piece beyond Jefferson, but I never knowed it was no eighty miles. So I stood there on that empty square, with daylight coming and coming and the street lights still burning and that Law looking down at me, and me still eighty miles from Memphis, and it had took me all night to walk jest twenty-two miles, and so, by the time I got to Memphis at that rate, Pete would 'a' done already started for Pearl Harbor.

"Where do you come from?" the Law said.

And I told him again. "I got to get to Memphis. My brother's there."

"You mean you ain't got any folks around here?" the Law said. "Nobody but that brother? What are you doing way off down here and your brother in Memphis?"

And I told him again, "I got to get to Memphis. I ain't got no time to waste talking about it and I ain't got time to walk it. I got to git there today."

"Come on here," the Law said.

We went down another street. And there was the bus, just like when Pete got into it yestiddy morning, except there wasn't no lights on it now and it was empty. There was a regular bus dee-po like a railroad dee-po, with a ticket counter and a feller behind it, and the Law said, "Set down over there," and I set down on the bench, and the Law said, "I want to use your telephone," and he talked in the telephone a minute and put it down and said to the feller behind the ticket counter, "Keep your eye on him. I'll be back as soon as Mrs. Habersham can arrange to get herself up and dressed." He went out. I got up and went to the ticket counter.

"I want to go to Memphis," I said.

"You bet," the feller said. "You set down on the bench now. Mr. Foote will be back in a minute."

"I don't know no Mr. Foote," I said. "I want to ride that bus to Memphis."

"You got some money?" he said. "It'll cost you seventy-two cents."

I taken out the matchbox and unwropped the shikepoke egg. "I'll swap you this for a ticket to Memphis," I said.

"What's that?" he said.

"It's a shikepoke egg," I said. "You never seen one before. It's worth a dollar. I'll take seventy-two cents fer it."

"No," he said, "the fellers that own that bus insist on a cash basis. If I started swapping tickets for bird eggs and livestock and such, they would fire me. You go and set down on the bench now, like Mr. Foote——"

I started for the door, but he caught me, he put one hand on the ticket counter and jumped over it and caught up with me and reached his hand out to ketch my shirt. I whupped out my pocketknife and snapped it open.

"You put a hand on me and I'll cut it off," I said.

I tried to dodge him and run at the door, but he could move quicker than any grown man I ever see, quick as Pete almost. He cut me off and stood with his back against the door and one foot raised a little, and there wasn't no other way to get out. "Get back on that bench and stay there," he said.

And there wasn't no other way out. And he stood there with his back against the door. So I went back to the bench. And then it seemed to me that dee-po was full of folks. There was that Law again, and there was two ladies in fur coats and their faces already painted. But they still looked like they had got up in a hurry and they still never liked it, a old one and a young one, looking down at me.

"He hasn't got an overcoat!" the old one said. "How in the world did he ever get down here by himself?"

"I ask you," the Law said. "I couldn't get nothing out of him except his brother is in Memphis and he wants to get back up there."

"That's right," I said. "I got to git to Memphis today."

"Of course you must," the old one said. "Are you sure you can find your brother when you get to Memphis?"

"I reckon I can," I said. "I ain't got but one and I have knowed him all my life. I reckon I will know him again when I see him."

The old one looked at me. "Somehow he doesn't look like he lives in Memphis," she said.

"He probably don't," the Law said. "You can't tell though. He might live anywhere, overhalls or not. This day and time they get scattered overnight from hope to breakfast; boys and girls, too, almost before they can walk good. He might have been in Missouri or Texas either yestiddy, for all we know. But he don't seem to have any doubt his brother is in Memphis. All I know to do is send him up there and leave him look."

"Yes," the old one said.

The young one set down on the bench by me and opened a hand satchel and taken out a artermatic writing pen and some papers.

"Now, honey," the old one said, "we're going to see that you find your brother, but we must have a case history for our files first. We want to know your name and your brother's name and where you were born and when your parents died."

"I don't need no case history neither," I said. "All I want is to get to Memphis. I got to get there today."

"You see?" the Law said. He said it almost like he enjoyed it. "That's what I told you."

"You're lucky, at that, Mrs. Habersham," the bus feller said. "I don't think he's got a gun on him, but he can open that knife fast enough to suit any man."

But the old one just stood there looking at me.

"Well," she said. "Well. I really don't know what to do."

"I do," the bus feller said. "I'm going to give him a ticket out of my own pocket, as a measure of protecting the company against riot and bloodshed. And when Mr. Foote tells the city board about it, it will be a civic matter and they will not only reimburse me, they will give me a medal too. Hey, Mr. Foote?"

But nobody paid him no mind. The old one still stood looking down at me. She said "Well," again. Then she taken a dollar from her purse and give it to the bus feller. "I suppose he will travel on a child's ticket, won't he?"

"Wellum," the bus feller said, "I just don't know what the regulations would be. Likely I will be fired for not crating him and marking the crate Poison. But I'll risk it."

Then they were gone. Then the Law come back with a sandwich and give it to me.

"You're sure you can find that brother?" he said.

"I ain't yet convinced why not," I said. "If I don't see Pete first, he'll see me. He knows me too."

Then the Law went out for good, too, and I et the sandwich. Then more folks come in and bought tickets, and then the bus feller said it was time to go, and I got into the bus just like Pete done, and we were gone.

I seen all the towns. I seen all of them. When the bus got to going good, I found out I was jest about wore out for sleep. But there was too much I hadn't never saw before. We run out of Jefferson and run past fields and woods, then we would run into another town and out of that un and past fields and woods again, and then into another town with stores and gins and water tanks, and we run along by the railroad for a spell and I seen the signal arm move, and then I seen the train and then some more towns, and I was jest about plumb wore out for sleep, but I couldn't resk it. Then Memphis begun. It seemed like, to me, it went on for miles. We would pass a patch of stores and I would think that was sholy it and the bus would even stop. But it wouldn't be Memphis yet and we would go on again past water tanks and smokestacks on top of the mills, and if they was gins and sawmills, I never knowed there was that many and I never seen any that big, and where they got enough cotton and logs to run um I don't know.

Then I seen Memphis. I knowed I was right this time. It was standing up into the air. It looked like about a dozen whole towns bigger than Jefferson was set up on one edge in a field, standing up into the air higher than ara hill in all Yoknapatawpha County. Then we was in it, with the bus stopping every few feet, it seemed like to me, and cars rushing past on both sides of it and the street crowded with folks from ever'where in town that day, until I didn't see how there could 'a' been nobody left in Mis'sippi a-tall to even sell me a bus ticket, let alone write out no case histories. Then the bus stopped. It was another bus dee-po, a heap bigger than the one in Jefferson. And I said, "All right. Where do folks join the army?"

"What?" the bus feller said.

And I said it again, "Where do folks join the army?"

"Oh," he said. Then he told me how to get there. I was afraid at first I wouldn't ketch on how to do in a town big as Memphis. But I caught on all right. I never had to ask but twice more. Then I was there, and I was durn glad to git out of all them rushing cars and shoving folks and all that racket fer a spell, and I thought, it won't be long now, and I thought how if there was any kind of a crowd there that had done already joined the army, too, Pete would likely see me before I seen him. And so I walked into the room. And Pete wasn't there.

He wasn't even there. There was a soldier with a big arrerhead on his sleeve, writing, and two fellers standing in front of him, and there was some more folks there, I reckon. It seems to me I remember some more folks there.

I went to the table where the soldier was writing, and I said, "Where's Pete?" and he looked up and I said, "My brother. Pete Grier. Where is he?"

"What?" the soldier said. "Who?"

And I told him again. "He joined the Army yestiddy. He's going to Pearl Harbor. So am I. I want to ketch him. Where you-all got him?" Now they were all looking at me, but I never paid them no mind. "Come on," I said. "Where is he?"

The soldier had quit writing. He had both hands spraddled out on the table. "Oh," he said. "You're going, too, hah?"

"Yes," I said. "They got to have wood and water. I can chop it and tote it. Come on. Where's Pete?"

The soldier stood up. "Who let you in here?" he said. "Go on. Beat it."

"Durn that," I said. "You tell me where Pete——"

I be dog if he couldn't move faster than the bus feller even. He never come over the table, he come around it, he was on me almost before I knowed it, so that I jest had time to jump back and whup out my pocket knife and snap it open and hit one lick, and he hollered and jumped back and grabbed one hand with the other hand and stood there cussing and hollering.

One of the other fellers grabbed me from behind, and I hit at him with the knife, but I couldn't reach him.

Then both of the fellers had me from behind, and then another soldier come out of a door at the back. He had on a belt with a britching strop over one shoulder.

"What's this?" he said.

"That little kid cut me with a knife!" the first soldier hollered. When he said that I tried to get at him again, but both them fellers was holding me, two against one, and the soldier with the backing strop said, "Here, here. Put your knife up, feller. None of us are armed. A man don't knife-fight folks that are barehanded." I could begin to hear him then. He sounded jest like Pete talked to me. "Let him go," he said. They let me go. "Now what's all the trouble about?" And I told him. "I see," he said. "And you come up to see if he was all right before he left."

"No," I said. "I come to________"

But he had already turned to where the first soldier was wropping a handkerchief around his hand.

"Have you got him?" he said. The first soldier went back to the table and looked at some papers.

"Here he is," he said. "He enlisted yestiddy. He's in a detachment leaving this morning for Little Rock." He had a watch stropped on his arm. He looked at it. "The train leaves in about fifty minutes. If I know country boys, they're probably all down there at the station right now."

"Get him up here," the one with the britching strop said. "Phone the station. Tell the porter to get him a cab. And you come with me," he said.

It was another office behind that un, with jest a table and some chairs. We set there while the soldier smoked, and it wasn't long; I knowed Pete's feet soon as I heard them. Then the first soldier opened the door and Pete come in. He never had no soldier clothes on. He looked jest like he did when he got on the bus yestiddy morning, except it seemed to me like it was at least a week, so much had happened, and I had done had to do so much traveling. He come in and there he was, looking at me like he hadn't never left home, except that here we was in Memphis, on the way to Pearl Harbor.

"What in durnation are you doing here?" he said.

And I told him, "You got to have wood and water to cook with. I can chop it and tote it for you-all."

"No," Pete said. "You're going back home."

"No, Pete," I said. "I got to go too. I got to. It hurts my heart, Pete."

"No," Pete said. He looked at the soldier. "I jest don't know what could have happened to him, looten-ant," he said. "He never drawed a knife on anybody before in his life."

He looked at me. "What did you do it for?"

"I don't know," I said. "I jest had to. I jest had to git here. I jest had to find you."

"Well, don't you never do it again, you hear?" Pete said. "You put that knife in your pocket and you keep it there. If I ever again hear of you drawing it on anybody, I'm coming back from wherever I am at and whup the fire out of you. You hear me?"

"I would pure cut a throat if it would bring you back to stay," I said. "Pete," I said. "Pete."

"No," Pete said. Now his voice wasn't hard and quick no more, it was almost quiet, and I knowed now I wouldn't never change him. "You must go home. You must look after maw, and I am depending on you to look after my ten acres. I want you to go back home. Today. Do you hear?"

"I hear," I said.

"Can he get back home by himself?" the soldier said.

"He come up here by himself," Pete said.

"I can get back, I reckon," I said. "I don't live in but one place. I don't reckon it's moved."

Pete taken a dollar out of his pocket and give it to

me. "That'll buy your bus ticket right to our mailbox," he said. "I want you to mind the lootenant. He'll send you to the bus. And you go back home and you take care of maw and look after my ten acres and keep that durn knife in your pocket. You hear me?"

"Yes, Pete," I said.

"All right," Pete said. "Now I got to go." He put his hand on my head again. But this time he never wrung my neck. He just laid his hand on my head a minute. And then I be dog if he didn't lean down and kiss me, and I heard his feet and then the door, and I never looked up and that was all, me setting there, rubbing the place where Pete kissed me and the soldier throwed back in his chair, looking out the window and coughing. He reached into his pocket and handed something to me without looking around. It was a piece of chewing gum.

"Much obliged," I said. "Well, I reckon I might as well start back. I got a right fer piece to go."

"Wait," the soldier said. Then he telephoned again and I said again I better start back, and he said again, "Wait. Remember what Pete told you."

So we waited, and then another lady come in, old, too, in a fur coat, too, but she smelled all right, she never had no artermatic writing pen nor no case history neither. She come in and the soldier got up, and she looked around quick until she saw me, and come and put her hand on my shoulder light and quick and easy as maw herself might 'a' done it.

"Come on," she said. "Let's go home to dinner."

"Nome," I said. "I got to ketch the bus to Jefferson."

"I know. There's plenty of time. We'll go home and eat dinner first."

She had a car. And now we was right down in the middle of all them other cars. We was almost under the busses, and all them crowds of people on the street close enough to where I could have talked to them if I had knowed who they was. After a while she stopped the car. "Here we are," she said, and I looked at it, and if all that was her house, she sho had a big family. But all of it wasn't. We crossed a hall with trees growing in it and went into a little room without nothing in it but a Negro dressed up in a uniform a heap shinier than them soldiers had, and the Negro shut the door, and then I hollered, "Look out!" and grabbed, but it was all right; that whole little room jest went right on up and stopped and the door opened and we was in another hall, and the lady unlocked a door and we went in, and there was another soldier, a old feller, with a britching strop, too, and a silver-colored bird on each shoulder.

"Here we are," the lady said. "This is Colonel McKellogg. Now, what would you like for dinner?"

"I reckon I'll jest have some ham and eggs and coffee," I said.

She had done started to pick up the telephone. She stopped. "Coffee?" she said. "When did you start drinking coffee?"

"I don't know," I said. "I reckon it was before I could remember."

"You're about eight, aren't you?" she said.

"Nome," I said. "I'm eight and ten months. Going on eleven months."

She telephoned then. Then we set there and I told them how Pete had jest left that morning for Pearl Harbor and I had aimed to go with him, but I would have to go back home to take care of maw and look after Pete's ten acres, and she said how they had a little boy about my size, too, in a school in the East. Then a Negro, another one, in a short kind of shirttail coat, rolled a kind of wheelbarrer in. It had my ham and eggs and a glass of milk and a piece of pie, too, and I thought

I was hungry. But when I taken the first bite I found out I couldn't swallow it, and I got up quick.

"I got to go," I said.

"Wait," she said.

"I got to go," I said.

"Just a minute," she said. "I've already telephoned for the car. It won't be but a minute now. Can't you drink the milk even? Or maybe some of your coffee?"

"Nome," I said. "I ain't hungry. I'll eat when I git home." Then the telephone rung. She never even answered it.

"There," she said. "There's the car." And we went back down in that 'ere little moving room with the dressed-up Negro. This time it was a big car with a soldier driving it. I got into the front with him. She give the soldier a dollar. "He might get hungry," she said. "Try to find a decent place for him."

"O.K., Mrs. McKellogg," the soldier said.

Then we was gone again. And now I could see Memphis good, bright in the sunshine, while we was swinging around it. And first thing I knowed, we was back on the same highway the bus run on this morning—the patches of stores and them big gins and sawmills, and Memphis running on for miles, it seemed like to me, before it begun to give out. Then we was running again between the fields and woods, running fast now, and except for that soldier, it was like I hadn't never been to Memphis a-tall. We was going fast now. At this rate, before I knowed it we would be home again, and I thought about me riding up to Frenchman's Bend in this big car with a soldier running it, and all of a sudden I begun to cry. I never knowed I was fixing to, and I couldn't stop it. I set there by that soldier, crying. We was going fast.

I Got a Name

Zachary Gold

My brother, Itzie, is a midget. Maybe not a midget exactly, but he's so small it counts for the same thing. Every time anybody looks at him, he throws his shoulders back and his chest out like he's going to blow up right through his skin. Even that doesn't help any.

But is that my fault? Did I make him that way?

Try to tell Itzie that.

He won't even listen. I never saw a kid who has less use for ears. You'd think he'd listen some of the time.

But no, not Itzie. Itzie always has to be right; Itzie always has to be talking. He's a regular Lippy Leo. Then he calls me a sorehead if I tell him to shut up; he thinks I'm picking on him. I should pick on midgets!

The kid says it's my fault everybody calls him Itzie. I did it; I always ride him he says. I'm the guy that made him small. Like I tried to tell Ma, it was Henny Prokesch who first called him Itzie. Henny said he was just an itsie-bitsie guy. Is that my fault? Can I go around telling people what to say?

God forbid I should happen to call him Itzie in the house. He begins screaming like the ceiling fell down on him. He begins calling me names I wouldn't take from anybody.

So does Ma tell him to keep his mouth shut? No. Ma tells me to call him Alfred. The whole world calls him Itzie; I should call him Alfred. Nobody even knows his name is Alfred.

"Does he call you anything but Frankie?" Ma says.

"You heard him," I say. "You heard what he called me."

"Don't change the subject," Ma says. "Your name is Frank and his is Alfred. You remember that."

So I began to call him Alfie in the house, and was that good enough? It had to be Alfred. I had to be careful, yet, how I said it. I had to be careful. I had to say it just right. Some kid.

He's half cracked, that's what he is. The kid's a little nuts. I never saw anybody, day in, day out, get out of bed on the wrong side like Itzie.

Every time you look at him, he's mad. Say something about the way he plays ball and bang!—he's sore. Say something about his brain or his size, and right away he's blowing steam like an engine. The whole world has brothers, but I have to get a nut like Itzie.

In the winter it isn't so bad because there's school then, but in the summer he's always hanging around.

"Why don't you leave him home?" the fellows say to me. "Why don't you tell him to go away?"

I should try to tell Itzie anything! For that matter, anybody should try. It gets you a swift nothing.

During the summer punchball is the big game. You can play punchball any place on the street. You play one sewer for home and the next sewer down the block for second; then halfway in between, on each side of the gutter, you lay out first and third, and you got a field. Then all you have to do is punch the ball out and play like baseball.

We got enough kids on the block for a couple of teams. This summer they picked me for captain of one of the teams, and when it came to choosing sides, it was me against Henny Prokesch.

So we chose and I got first pick. Naturally, because this wasn't something just for me, I tried to get the best guys. I mean it wasn't something where a fellow could play favorites. The first thing I had to look out for was that I get me a good team. I even picked Joey Lune, and I hate Joey. But he's the classiest firstbaseman on the block, and he hits a mean ball. So I wasn't just trying to keep Itzie out; I wanted him to get a game, but I had to pick the best guys first, didn't I?

It ended up with me having six guys and Henny having six guys and Itzie standing there on the curb waiting to be picked.

"Don't I get a game?" Itzie said. "What's the matter—am I an orphan?"

"I got my team," Henny said.

"That's fair! You radishes; you red and yellow radishes!"

"What are you getting sore about?" I said. "Take it easy."

"Sure. Sure. Take it easy. Every chump on the block gets a game, but I'm left out."

"You can warm up with the guys," Henny said. "You can do that, Itzie."

"I got a name," the kid said. "You call me Al."

He was getting sore. In another minute he would have been swinging at somebody.

"Listen," I said, "you'll play."

"Yeah?" Itzie said. "How? You show me how."

"Look. It's summer now and some of the kids'll be going away to the country a while, and some days they'll be going to the beach. Or maybe they'll get sick. You know how it is. There'll always be room for you. You'll always get a game."

"How about today?"

"Well, maybe not today," I said.

"That's some system," Itzie said. "I got to pray somebody breaks a leg."

But he knew what I meant, and I saw him cooling off, so I knew it was all right. You got to think fast with that kid around.

And sure enough, that's how it was. Itzie played nearly every game. In fact, he went out and bought a special high-bouncer ball for us to use. He used to bring the ball with him every time we played. We always used Itzie's ball.

One day one of my guys didn't show up, and Itzie played on my side. It was one tight game, believe me. Before we could say go, the other guys had plunked in three runs, and when we got up, we just couldn't do anything.

We held them all right after that, but we couldn't do a thing in our half of the inning. We were popping up flies to the outfield, and all our grounders were going smack into the hands of the infielders. We just couldn't do anything.

Then in the last inning Joey Lune got up and clouted a triple off McGrady's stoop, way down the block. It would have been a home run, only the outfielder made a lucky heave, and Joey had to hold it up at third.

We sacrificed him in, but that left us with two runs to tie and three to win. Then, all of a sudden, we began to hit. For the next four guys, three of them got on base, and one popped out. So it was two out and the winning run on first and Itzie up. My heart nearly dropped out because, between you and me, Itzie's not exactly a hitter. He can place a ball all right, but he has no power.

Itzie took his time and smacked a grounder down between second and third, and right away I saw it was good. Then, like it always happens, there was a break in the game and Henny himself made a wild throw to the plate, and three runs scored because the ball got lost in the hedges around the Elliot lawn.

Itzie got a clean single, all right, but the three runs were breaks. We deserved one, but not three. But that's how it goes, and I was so happy I nearly kissed the kid.

"Itzie," I said, "you're a wonder. That was some smack."

"Thanks," he said.

"You were right there in the clutch."

"I smacked it and prayed."

"It takes more than praying, and you got it," I said.

He was right in there with us, the kid was. And talking his head off. But it was all right. Sometimes you don't mind; it's all in how things are. Sometimes it sounds fresh and sometimes it doesn't. With that game under my belt, it sounded like music.

It was hot sitting on the stoop, and my mouth felt sticky and dry. I saw Henny giving me the wink and pointing to the corner. We could go around the block and get a soda or something. Henny could live on that stuff; I never saw a guy drink soda like Henny.

"It was lucky," Itzie was saying. "I just happened to see the hole and put it there. That's all. It was lucky."

I got up and walked over to Henny.

"How about a soda?" Henny said.

"O.K."

"We could stop in at Mahoney's and stick around a while. It's early yet."

"Sure," I said.

Mahoney's was a pool parlor next to the candy store. He wouldn't let us play, but he let us stand around and watch. He always got the baseball scores first, too.

"Where you going, Frankie?" the kid said when he saw me walking away.

"Just around," I said.

He got up.

"Where you think you're going?" I said.

"With you."

That's it all the time. You're nice to the kid, and right away he thinks he's your shadow. Sure, I should let him come along and take him with me to Mahoney's. Next thing I'd know he'd go blah-blah-blah to Mom about Mahoney's. That kid just doesn't know when he's had enough.

"Not with me, you ain't going," I said.

You should have seen him. Like I kicked him or something. Everything I do, I got to worry about him.

"What do you mean, I ain't going?" he said. "Everybody's going."

"Not you," I said.

Right away he got mad. Right away King Itzie was in

a temper. "The sidewalk's free. You ain't got a lease on the sidewalk. I can go where I want, can't I?"

"Not with me," I said.

"I'm going."

"Go on home, peewee."

For a minute I thought he was going to fight or argue some more. But he just stood there looking like I took his last nickel. "You're some brother," he said. "You're some lousy brother."

Then he turned and ran the other way down the block.

I had a plain chocolate at the candy store, and we stayed a while kidding around. Then when we figured it would be around the sixth inning, we went over to Mahoney's.

We stuck around Mahoney's, watching the boys shoot pool. The things some of those guys can do! It's like a free education down at Mahoney's.

The Dodgers scored in the seventh, but it didn't help any. In the other half of the inning, the other guys scored twice. I get good and sick and tired of those Dodgers sometimes.

I could see the game was as good as over, so I gave Henny the high sign and we got out.

I trotted down the block and all the way home. I was puffing when I got to the door. I got upstairs and headed for the bathroom to wash up. I knew Ma would be sore because I was so late. I thought if I could get into the bathroom, maybe Ma would cool off by the time I got out. But Ma heard me, and she came walking out of the bedroom. "Is Alfred with you?" she said.

"With me? He ain't been with me since this afternoon."

"Hasn't," Ma said.

"Anyway, I don't know where he is."

"Didn't he play with you this afternoon?"

"Sure. Sure," I said.

"Where did you go after the game?"

"Oh, just around."

"And what about Alfred?"

"How should I know, Ma? Tell me, how should I know?"

Ma was worried. "Where could he be?" she said.

"I don't know," I said. "I can go out and look. Maybe he's just hanging around somewheres."

"All right," Pa said. "Go out and look. But come back in a half hour. Don't stay out any longer. Do you understand?"

"Sure," I said. "Half hour."

I climbed into a sweater and went out. Ma looked awfully worried.

I walked up and down the block twice. He wasn't anywheres around. I even looked in the alleys. Who knows where a crazy kid like that could be? I tried near the schoolyard around the corner. Sometimes a gang of kids hangs out near the school at night. Why anyone should want to go near the place in vacation, I don't know; but they do anyway. Itzie wasn't there.

There was no place else to look, so I started home again. I came into our block and right there ahead of me I could see the kid walking. He must have come down from the parkway. He hadn't passed me, and there was no other place he could have come from.

I trotted and caught up with him.

"Where you been?" I said.

He didn't answer me; he just kept walking.

"You dopey nut," I said. "Ma's worried sick. Where you been?"

Go talk to a wall. I could have socked him. He didn't say anything, not a word. He wouldn't even look at me.

Worrying Ma like that and then marching up like he was King Kong or something. He deserved a sock. He deserved a good slamming.

"Well?" I said. "You talking? Or do I have to give you a smack?"

He began to run. I chased after him. He got to the house before I did and slammed the door in my face. By the time I got upstairs, he was in the bedroom. Pa was sitting at the kitchen table, and Ma was inside with Itzie.

"Where were you?" I heard Ma say.

"Just out."

"What happened?"

"Nothing."

"Something happened," Ma said. "What?"

"Nothing."

"Tell me. I promise I won't be angry."

"Do you want me to tell your father to come in? Would you like that?"

"I don't care. I don't care. I don't care."

Then I heard something, like he was crying. That kid. What happened to him?

Ma came out and sat down at the table. "Let's eat," she said. Pa was looking at her, but she didn't say a word more.

That was some meal. We sat there like a bunch of dummies, nobody saying anything, just on account of a snotty kid.

After supper I did some reading and then sat around listening to the radio. Itzie didn't come out once. He didn't even come out for something to eat. He just stayed in the bedroom. At eleven o'clock I called it a night and went in to undress.

Itzie was already in bed. He looked like he was asleep, but he wasn't. I could tell.

"Itzie," I said. "Itzie."

He wouldn't answer.

I got undressed and climbed into bed. I tried again.

"Hey, Al–"

I should bat my head against a stone wall. I went to sleep.

I don't know what woke me. I can sleep even if a bunch of elephants comes stamping into the room. But that night something woke me up, and I opened my eyes, and I saw Pa sitting on Itzie's bed, talking to him.

I didn't let on I was awake. I didn't say anything. I kept my eyes closed, but I could hear them talking.

"Nothing," Itzie said.

"What happened after the game?" Pa said.

"We just sat around. That's all."

"Did you do something wrong? Did you make an error?"

"No. Gee, I was good. I was real good."

"What happened, then?"

"Nothing. Honest."

"Did Frankie say something to you?"

"Frankie didn't do anything."

"Where did Frankie go after the game?"

"He went away somewheres with Henny. I don't know."

"Didn't you go along?"

"No."

"What about the rest of the fellows?"

"They all went."

"Why didn't you go?"

"I don't know. I just felt like sitting around."

"Did Frankie tell you not to go?"

Itzie didn't say anything.

"Is that what happened?" Pa said. "Did Frankie say something to you?"

He wouldn't answer. He didn't say a word.

"I'll talk to Frankie tomorrow," Pa said.

I just laid there thinking. I get blamed for everything. It was my fault. Pa thought I was to blame. That Itzie! Of all the people in the world, I get a kid like Itzie for a brother. He was poison, that's what he was. Every time anything happened, I got blamed. If it was going to be that way, let him keep away from me; let him stop hanging around. I'd show him, all right; he'd see.

In the morning I waited until Pa was gone before I got out of bed. Then I dressed and ate breakfast and got out into the street. All the guys were there waiting for the punchball game. Itzie was over by the house, banging the high-bouncer against the stoop.

Like the other day, one of my guys was missing. We got up in two teams, and I saw Itzie coming over. He stood near the outside of the circle.

"All right," I said good and loud, "we'll play you one man short."

"What about me?" Itzie said. "Don't I get a game?"

That's what I was waiting for. "What about you?" I said. "You're no regular."

"It's all right with the other guys," Itzie said. "They say it's O.K."

"Go on home," I said. "Go away."

"I'm playing," Itzie said.

"I said no."

"Don't tell me what to do."

"I'm telling you you're not playing."

"You can't stop me. You're one man short and I'm playing. You said so yourself."

Sure, I said so once. So any time anything happens, I get blamed. I should always take the rap for him. Not me. Let him take care of himself for a change.

"We don't need anybody else," I said. "Throw the

ball over here and keep score if you want to do something."

"Yeah?" he said. "Yeah?"

"Yeah," I said. "Throw the ball over."

"Either I play or no ball," Itzie said.

"Listen to him. Listen to the shrimp. Should I come over and take it away?"

"You got to catch me first, big flat feet."

"Throw it over before I get sore."

"I play."

"I told you no."

"No ball then."

"Throw it over."

"Yah! Come and get it."

Itzie was dancing in the street, hopping up and down. I stepped in to him. He danced back. I grabbed, but he was like oil. He was off in a second and I chased him.

He ran around cars and dodged up alleys and across lawns. I nearly got him a couple of times, but he was too shifty and quick. I couldn't get close enough to him.

Then he ran up to the stoop of our house and stood on the top step with his back against the door. "Balloon belly, come and catch me!"

I was standing in the middle of the gutter, good and sore. The little wise guy!

"I'll go and get another ball," Henny said.

"We'll play with that one," I said.

Then I told the fellows to surround the stoop and, when I gave the word, to close in. I was through playing games with him.

I started toward the steps. Itzie had a rock in his hand. He hefted it and yelled: "I'll bean the first guy that comes near me!"

You should have seen his face. It was like a sheet.

"Throw the ball over," I said.

"I swear I'll bean you!" Itzie yelled.

"Give me that ball."

I kept walking in, and when I got to the steps, Itzie pulled his arm back, and I saw the rock coming at me. I tried to duck, but it was too late. I felt like my head was split open. I was down on the sidewalk holding my face. There was blood all over my hands. Itzie was standing on the steps; he looked scared. Suddenly he threw the ball at me. It bounced in the gutter and rolled away.

I tried to get up, but I couldn't. I heard Henny yell once, and then I didn't hear anything at all.

The doctor took three stitches in my face, and I thought my cheek was going to fall off. Ma kept me in bed, but I felt all right.

When Pa came home, Itzie got it hot and heavy. That kid sure had it coming to him.

But when I was in bed, I got to thinking. Can you imagine the shrimp doing that to me—heaving a rock? It's like that with the kids on the block. Sometimes you'll stick your chest right up against somebody and say, "Go ahead, do something!" and he'll say, "Go ahead, you do something, I dare you!"

And you'll stand there and talk, but it takes an awful lot before you'll start swinging. It takes a lot of nerve to heave a rock; a fellow has to feel pretty bad before he'll do anything like that.

Even Ma was down on Itzie. She brought him into the room. "Tell Frank you're sorry," she said.

"Aw, Ma—" I said.

"Go ahead," she said to Itzie.

The kid stood there a minute. "I didn't mean to hurt him," he said. "But I'm not sorry. He asked for it, that's what he did. He's some brother."

Can you imagine that? Right after Pa got through

with him too. You have to beat that kid's brains out before he learns anything. Some guy.

"Alfred—" Ma said.

"I won't. I won't."

"All right," Ma said. "No more ball playing for you. You stay in the house every day for a week. You learn how to behave before you go out to play again. Throwing rocks! And at your own brother."

The kid didn't say a word.

In the morning Ma made pancakes for breakfast, and she kept piling them on my plate until I thought I'd bust. The kid didn't even seem hungry.

It was a real swell day; not too hot, not too cold. Ma didn't say, but I could see she was waiting for Itzie to say something. But no, not Itzie; that kid hasn't got any sense. He gets me sore.

So, for Ma's sake, because I could see she was feeling pretty bad, I said: "It was an accident, Mom. He didn't mean it. You let him go out, and if he does anything wrong, I'll ship him right back upstairs."

Ma looked at Itzie and she looked at me, and finally she said, "Well—but remember, Alfred, whatever Frank says goes."

We went downstairs together, and you'd think he'd say thanks or something to me. Not that kid. I'm not asking any favors, but he could do a little thing like that.

The whole gang was outside on the stoop. I could see the way they were looking at Itzie. They were a little scared of him. All of a sudden, he was different. Some of them didn't even see the bandage on my cheek.

"Hiya, Frankie," Henny said. "How's the face?"

"Just a couple of stitches," I said. "Nothing."

"Hiya, Itzie," Henny said.

Go ask me why I did it. When bigger dopes are born, they won't have anything on me.

"He's got a name," I said to Henny. "Call him Al."

Here I've been calling him Itzie as long as I can remember; out of nowhere I become a big-hearted Joe.

"Hey, Al," I called, "come on, walk me down, and we'll take a look at yesterday's scores in Mahoney's."

That was me talking. When I go crazy, I go the whole hog, all right.

You should have seen the kid.

About halfway down the block, I said, "What do you think of the Dodgers for next year, Al?"

"Look, Frankie," the kid said. "Call me Itzie, will you?"

Go figure it out.

Husbands and Wives

Husbands and wives
   With children between them
Sit in the subway;
   So I have seen them.

One word only
   From station to station;
So much talk for
   So close a relation.

Miriam Hershenson

Overstatement is exaggerating a fact in order to point out an irony: something contrary to what's expected. What's the irony here?

The Undercurrent

Fay Ehlert

The scene is a basement kitchen which also does duty as living and dining room in an old-fashioned New York apartment building. An air of orderliness pervades the room, which is furnished with the meager belongings of the FISHYER *family. Shabby, faded curtains hang limply on each side of the small, iron-barred window in the left wall. The galvanized sink is in the back, flanked on the right by the kitchen range and on the left by an old cupboard. A coat rack has been nailed to the side of this cupboard. Over the sink is a shelf, holding an alarm clock, comb and brush, and shaving mug. The kitchen table, covered with a red tablecloth, occupies almost the exact center of the room. Upon the table are four plates, knives, forks, cups and saucers, half a loaf of rye bread, a glass jar filled with teaspoons, and a partly filled bottle of milk. There are four chairs around the table.*

To the left of this table and near the front of the room stands a dilapidated horsehair sofa. Directly across from this sofa on the right side of the room is a Morris chair which through long usage has sagged and remolded itself to PA FISHYER'S *two hundred odd pounds. The door in the right wall leads into a short corridor through which the* FISHYERS *must pass in order to reach the bedrooms, boiler room, storeroom, back stairs, etc. A small table, laden with pipes, tobacco jar, and the Bible, is on one side of this door, and the wall phone on the other. A clothesline with its motley array of rags has been fastened to a hook above the phone and then stretched diagonally across the stove to the shelf above the sink. As this room is below street level, it is necessary to mount a short flight of stairs in the left wall in order to reach the areaway door.*

It is evening, about five minutes of six, and a light snow is falling. The feet of the passers-by can be seen through the dimly frosted windowpanes.

MA FISHYER *is peering through the window. Her whole attitude is one of terrible anxiety and she turns with a half sob of relief as she hears the areaway door open stealthily.*

Ma Fishyer *(under her breath):* A-annie?

Mrs. Floyd *(stalking down the stairs):* Hello, there!

Ma Fishyer *(swallowing her disappointment):* Ach, it's yuh, Mis' Floyd! I-I thought yuh vas *(she turns back to the window again)* s-somebody else!

Mrs. Floyd *(maliciously):* Didya now! *(Eyes* ANNIE'S *place at table.)* Who, fer instance?

Ma Fishyer: Ach, eferybody alvays comes to de jeniter for something–maybe Mis' Richards about de g-garbage pails–

Mrs. Floyd: . . . or mebbe even Annie, huh?

Ma Fishyer *(unaware of the other's curt smile):* Shure, it's Thursday today, and she always comes–

Mrs. Floyd: Is that so? Well, ya never kin tell! *(Shakes fist at door to corridor.)* Huh, I got some news to spill in yer ear! *(Seats herself in* PA FISHYER'S *chair, at the table.)*

Ma Fishyer: Ach, not–not now! *(Still peering out of window.)* Pa'll be here right avay and by six he vants to eat. Not a minute efter six vill he vait– *(She looks at the clock.)*

Mrs. Floyd *(leaning over):* It's about someone ya know!

Ma Fishyer: . . . and ef Annie ain't here on time– *(She turns, startled, as* MRS. FLOYD'S *last words reach her.)* A-about somevun vat I know–vat I kn-know?

Mrs. Floyd *(venting her spite):* I'll tell de world ya do!

Ma Fishyer: It ain't nothin' bad?

Mrs. Floyd: Bad? Well! *(She glares at the door to corridor.)* I imagine some people what thinks *my* son ain't good company fer their daughter–certainly are going to have a fit tonight! *(With compressed lips.)* I'll say *he* is! Yes, siree!

Ma Fishyer *(coming slowly towards her):* It ain't 'bout Annie?

Mrs. Floyd: Nuthin' else but!

Ma Fishyer *(moans):* Ach! *(Goes fearfully toward door to corridor and, half opening it, listens intently.)*

Mrs. Floyd: My son may be a little wild, but he ain't never been *arrested* yet.

Ma Fishyer: Arrest– *(She darts forward and puts her hand over* MRS. FLOYD'S *mouth.)* Shhhh!

Mrs. Floyd *(sputtering):* Say–

Ma Fishyer *(she glances terror-stricken to door):* Pleese to go now–he-he's comin', h-he's c-comin'!

Mrs. Floyd: What of it? I ain't skeered of him.

Ma Fishyer: P-pleese, not now! *(Desperately.)* Not now–come efter vile–pleese– *(Tugs at her dress.)*

Mrs. Floyd *(rising):* All right! I'll go! *(Shakes her off.)* But stop pushing! I'm going! *(Hobbles up the stairs and slams door. Before* MA FISHYER *can breathe her relief, she opens the door again.)* But I'll be back later!

Ma Fishyer: Yess, yess, l-later–

(Scarcely has the door closed after MRS. FLOYD *when* PA FISHYER *enters wearily from corridor.)*

Fishyer *(throwing his denim jacket over Morris chair):* Huh! *(He strides over to the sink and begins washing himself.)* Huh! Supper ready?

Ma Fishyer *(at the table):* A-almost–

Fishyer *(he growls):* Almost? Don'tcha know yess or no? *(He pushes up his spectacles and glares at the clock.)* Vere's Annie? It's nearly six already!

Ma Fishyer: De c-clock iss a l-little f-fest– *(Walks nervously to window.)*

Fishyer: Fest? Dat clock iss *alvays* right, you hear me? Alvays right!

Ma Fishyer: Yess, P-pa!

Fishyer *(his wrath increasing):* Vell, vere iss she?

Ma Fishyer *(busies herself at stove):* Na, Pa, she'll be h-here eny minute soon! Yuh know h-how de l-lady k-keeps her! *(She glances at the door through which* MRS. FLOYD *has left.)* And m-maybe–in dis b-bed veather, she kent come at all!

Fishyer: Vat! *(Drying his hands.)*

Ma Fishyer: I–I mean–efen in *good* veather, only vunce a veek does she haff a day off.

Fishyer: Dat'll do! *(Throws towel on sink.)* Ve vait till six *(takes Bible from table and seats himself in Morris chair)* and den ve eat! *(Groans as he rubs his rheumatic left arm.* EMIL *enters.)* Na, Dummy, vat did she vant? *(Points upward.)*

Emil *(timidly):* She fergot her key and–

Fishyer: . . . and yuh hed to open de door for her! *(He growls.)* Vy don't yuh say dat right avay? *(He begins reading the Bible, following each word with his finger.)*

Ma Fishyer: Come, Emil *(she nods warningly in* FISHYER'S *direction)* and vash yerself.

Fishyer *(he reads laboriously):* "Train op a child in de vay he should go" *(glares at* EMIL *and then repeats)* "de vay he *should* go!" *(Reads.)* ". . . and ven he iss old" *(repeats to himself)* "old–he vill not depart from it–"

(There is a knock at the outer door and MA FISHYER *stands transfixed, her face ashen.* EMIL, *his hands half-washed, looks inquiringly at his father.)*

Fishyer: Na, open de door!

Emil *(hurriedly wiping his hands on his trousers, he mounts the steps and opens the door):* Whatcha want?

Miss Page: Good evening! Does Annie Fishyer live here?

Emil: Yeh– *(he shuffles back to the sink)* –come on in!

Miss Page *(descending the stairs):* Thank you. I wasn't quite sure. *(Kindly to* MA FISHYER.) You must be Annie's mother and–

Fishyer: I em Karl Fishyer!

Miss Page: Ah, yes, Annie's father. *(She smiles her quick, warm smile.)* I don't think you know me. I am Miss Page, a special investigator from the Morals Court!

Ma Fishyer *(tremulously to* FISHYER): De lady, Pa, de l-lady vat Annie v-vorks f-for–

Fishyer: So?

Miss Page *(surprised):* Works for me?

Ma Fishyer *(hurriedly):* Pleese to come and sit down, mis', here on de sofa! *(She deftly dusts the sofa with a swish of her apron and then steps back and looks at* MISS PAGE *apprehensively.)*

Miss Page: I think you are mistaking me– *(She stops as she sees* MA FISHYER'S *drawn face.)*

Ma Fishyer *(indicating the sofa):* P-pleese, mis'—

(PA FISHYER *meanwhile replaces the Bible on the table.* MISS PAGE *sits down without another word.)*

Ma Fishyer *(quickly):* Annie a-ain't home yet, b-but—

Miss Page *(puzzled):* Isn't home yet? Are you expecting her?

Fishyer: Huh? *(He turns towards them.)* Shure, I expect her to come!

Ma Fishyer: Y-yess, she always c-c-comes here on her day off—Pa means!

Miss Page *(probing gently):* Her day off?

Ma Fishyer: Maybe she n-nefer tells yuh, b-but she alvays c-c-comes here Thursdays. *(She wets her lips.)* D-don't she, Pa?

Fishyer *(grudgingly):* Huh! *(To* MISS PAGE.) Since she's vid yuh, mis', yess!

Ma Fishyer *(she talks to* MISS PAGE, *but her eyes are anxiously on* FISHYER): And efery cent vat she earns by yuh, she brings to her pa!

Miss Page: She—does what? *(Drawing off her gloves.)*

Ma Fishyer: E-efery cent she brings to her pa! She iss a fine girl—

Fishyer *(cutting her short):* Vat's dot to brag ofer?

Miss Page *(soothingly): Well,* I'm sure Annie is—

Ma Fishyer *(eagerly):* Yuh hear, Pa? Efen Mis' Page sez vat a fine Annie ve got.

Fishyer: Huh, she's purty goot *now!* But before she vent mit yuh, mis' *(he clenches his fist in wrath) I*—her fadder—didn't know vhere she vas for three month efen—(MISS PAGE *suppresses a start.)*

Ma Fishyer *(imploringly):* But, Pa, yuh know *now* vere she vas! *(To* MISS PAGE.) H-he m-means de time ven she v-vas by yuh in *(she swallows hard)* de *country.*

(MISS PAGE *conceals her astonishment.)*

Fishyer: Efen ef she vas—

Ma Fishyer: . . . and how vell she looked ven—

Fishyer: . . . she come home agen! *(He paces angrily back and forth.)* I hear dot a million times already, too!

Ma Fishyer: But, P-pa—

Fishyer: All I say iss—dot's no vay to treat yur fadder! And efter de strict bringing op I giff de children, dey must remember—alvays—dat I em dere fadder! *I em de boss here! (To* EMIL, *crouching against the wall.)* Yuh hear me?

Ma Fishyer *(imploringly):* Pa, pleese, Pa.

Fishyer *(glaring at the clock):* It's six, ve eat now! *(He seats himself at table and begins slicing bread, motions* EMIL *to his seat.* EMIL *sits facing the audience.)*

Miss Page *(she has been watching them attentively):* Yes, don't let me interrupt you!

Fishyer: I alvays eat at six! *(Turns towards stove.)* Vere iss dot girl? (MA *comes to table with platter of stew, which she places quickly before him.)* Vat time yuh let her come today, mis'—?

(Before she can answer, steps are heard and ANNIE *enters hurriedly from the areaway door.)*

Fishyer: Dere she iss! *(Points at her with knife.)*

Annie *(breathlessly):* Oh, Pa, I couldn't—I couldn't help it, I wuz— *(She sees* EMIL'S *finger surreptitiously signaling* MISS PAGE'S *presence. She gives* MISS PAGE *a terror-stricken look, then shrinks back against the wall for support.)*

Annie *(gasps):* Oh!

Ma Fishyer *(she goes toward her quickly, and holding her tight against her breast, speaks so as to give her time to recover):* Ach, no vunder she iss surprised to see her lady here!

Annie *(clinging to her):* Ma!

Miss Page *(slowly, with great significance):* I had an errand to do in this neighborhood, Annie, and as I passed this house, I stopped in *(sees* MA FISHYER'S *pleading look)* to—to get acquainted with your parents!

Fishyer: And ve are gled to know yuh also. *(He motions to the table.)* Yuh eat mit us?

(EMIL *pushes out* ANNIE'S *chair for her.)*

Miss Page: No, thank you. If you don't mind, I'll just sit here.

Fishyer: Shure! Make yurself to home. *(He bangs on the table with his knife.)* Ma, ve eat now!

(ANNIE *hangs her coat and hat on coat rack.)*

Fishyer *(motioning to* ANNIE): Sit down!

(ANNIE *slips into her chair, facing her father.* MA FISHYER *brings coffeepot to table.)*

Miss Page *(observing* EMIL *with interest):* I didn't know Annie had a brother.

Ma Fishyer *(hurriedly, before* FISHYER *can answer):* Ach, yess, and sotch a good boy! He helps his pa take care off de house.

Fishyer *(grudgingly):* Huh!

Ma Fishyer *(dishing out the food to* EMIL *and* ANNIE): And someday he'll be a jeniter, too! And like our coffee man sez: "Jeniter vork iss nuthin' to sneeze at!" So vat vid Pa's rheumatism, ve are gled to haff Emil help so nice!

Fishyer: Emil—bahhh! (EMIL *crouches behind his mother's arm.)*

Ma Fishyer: And yuh haff no idea, mis', how mutch vork dere iss here to do! *(Pours coffee.)* So vid our Emil—

(FISHYER *laughs derisively.)*

Miss Page *(soothingly):* Yes, you must be kept very busy, Mr. Fishyer!

Fishyer: Bizzy? Yuh don't know it, mis', how crazy *(he points upward with his knife)* dose vomens get me! First, vun comes and sez de vater iss too hot—dat efery time she turns it on, she a Turkish bath gets! Den— *(The phone rings.)* Yuh see, not efen peace on a meal I got— *(Pushes back his chair.)*

Ma Fishyer: Vait, Pa, I go! *(She hurries to phone.)* Hollo! Yess, Mis' Richards, yess, he *iss* by de boiler (PA FISHYER *motions for* EMIL *to go out)* puttin' more coal on! Yess, mam! *(She turns from phone just in time to see* EMIL'S *scowling gesture at his father's back.)* Emil! (EMIL *grabs his cap in frantic haste.)* Yur cap— *(Pushes him toward door.)* Quick!

(PA FISHYER, *unaware of what is passing in back of his chair, pounds the table emphatically with his fist. With a terrified look,* EMIL *rushes out, letting* MA FISHER *close the door behind him.)*

Fishyer *(he raises his head stubbornly):* I tell yuh, dat voman could by de devil sit and yet be cold!

Ma Fishyer: Yess, yess, Pa! But ve are gled to haff dis job! And vat—mit our Emil and Annie helpin' so nice—

Fishyer: Helpin'! Bahhhh!

Ma Fishyer: Ach, Mis' Page, efery night I thank de good Gott for my Annie—

Annie *(turns quickly and gives her mother a beseeching glance):* Ma—oh, M-ma— *(Her coffee cup falls from her nerveless hand, spilling its contents on her dress.)*

Fishyer: Huh!

Annie: Pa—P-pa—it slipped! I—I'll change my dress! *(She rushes out door to bedroom.)*

Fishyer *(looks after her):* Huh! *(Accuses* MA FISHYER *while he dips his bread in his coffee.)* Fine manners she got!

(Phone rings again.)

Ma Fishyer *(running to phone):* Yess, yess, Mis' Richards! *(Into receiver.)* Hollo— Yess, Mis' Richards, he *iss—*

Fishyer *(exasperated):* Oh, vat a dummy of a son I got! *(To* MA FISHYER.) Maybe he fell in de coal bin again! *(Exits, rubbing his rheumatic left arm.)*

(MA FISHYER *turns from the phone, listens a moment at the door through which* PA FISHYER *has gone, then quickly crosses the room to* MISS PAGE. *Her whole manner has changed; she seems to have shrunk suddenly.)*

Ma Fishyer: I em gled to know yuh, mis'! *(She clasps and unclasps her hands.)* And my Annie—my Annie—

Miss Page *(gently):* Sit down, Mrs. Fishyer!

Ma Fishyer *(she sinks down in* ANNIE'S *chair at the table):* She—she iss mit y-yuh?

Miss Page *(compassionately):* In a way—yes.

Ma Fishyer: In a vay?

Miss Page: Yes, I am interested in her welfare and am looking after her.

Ma Fishyer *(scarcely audible):* S-she don't live m-mit yuh?

Miss Page: Not exactly—

Ma Fishyer: Ach, don't tell dis to Pa! *(In despair.)* Pleese, pleese, don't tell him enyding vat iss agenst her!

Miss Page *(leaning forward):* I don't understand.

Ma Fishyer: If—if he knows eferyding *(swallowing with difficulty)* h-he kills her!

Miss Page *(gently):* Do *you* know everything about her?

Ma Fishyer *(terrified):* No, no, don't tell me! Pleese not to tell me! I don't vant to know!

Miss Page: Not even when you may be able to help her?

Ma Fishyer *(shaking her head):* All I kin do *(motioning to the boiler room)* iss to keep *him* from findin' out d-dings about her! *(She looks her full in the face.)* I don't vant to know enyding agenst my Annie!

Miss Page *(puzzled):* But if you remain in ignorance, how can you be of assistance?

Ma Fishyer *(tremulously):* I kin help her only by—knowin' nodding.

Miss Page: What do you mean? You as her mother should be anxious to know.

Ma Fishyer: Yess, yuh haff right! But yuh don't know Pa! *(She whispers.)* He alvays suspicions eferybody! Me—Emil—Annie! He dinks I hide from him someding about de children! *(She pauses.)* And den—it best iss I don't know dings. *(Slowly.)* Ven yuh don't know dings, he kent be scoldin' yuh all de time!

Miss Page *(aghast):* But—why should he?

Ma Fishyer *(bitterly):* Ach, vy! Vy should he? *(She passes her hand across her eyes.)* Vat kin yuh do mit a man vat hass in his head only *vun idea!*

Miss Page: One idea?

Ma Fishyer: Vun idea! *(Brokenly.)* Dot all children should be brought op *strict*—mit mutch scoldin' and vhippin'.

Miss Page *(indignantly):* But can't you convince him that such harsh methods—

Ma Fishyer *(sobs):* I k-kin do nodding mit him—no vun kin! *(She beats her clenched fist against her forehead.)* He hass dot vun idea in his head and *(she stares frantically at the door through which* MRS. FLOYD *has gone)* h-he must n-nefer find out!

Miss Page: Find out what? *(As* MA FISHYER *rocks back and forth, weeping.)* Don't be afraid. Tell me.

Ma Fishyer *(tearfully):* Pleese, Mis' Page, don't let him find out dings a-agenst A-Annie! *(Weeps.)* P-p-pleese, pleese, see I go on m-my knees t-to yuh! *(Sinks down at* MISS PAGE'S *knees.)* Pleese—p-p-pleese!

Miss Page *(her eyes filled with tears):* Don't cry, don't! *(She places her arm around* MA FISHYER'S *shaking shoulders.)* Why didn't you come to see me?

Ma Fishyer *(weeping as she grasps* MISS PAGE'S *hands in agony):* Ach, I vanted to c-come so m-meny t-times and esk yuh—take c-care off Annie! L-look efter her—b-but I vas afraid!

Miss Page: Afraid?

Ma Fishyer: Yess, because—m-maybe—

Miss Page *(she looks with sudden understanding toward* ANNIE'S *chair):* . . . there *was* no Miss Page?

Ma Fishyer: Yess! But n-now I seen yuh! *(She grasps* MISS PAGE'S *arms convulsively.)* Yuh *vill* l-look out for her, von't yuh? *(She wails.)* It iss all I haff in de vorld—my two c-children—all I haff. *(Sinks, weeping bitterly, against* MISS PAGE.)

(EMIL'S *whimpering cry is heard from the boiler room.)*

Emil: M-ma! Oh, Ma!

Ma Fishyer *(she starts up):* It's Emil! Yuh vill oxcuse me? *(Wearily.)* I gotta go—he forgot agen to open de valve maybe! *(She grabs her shawl from the coat rack.)* And Pa mit hiss rheumatism kent reach op—

(MISS PAGE *rises.)*

Fishyer *(angrily from the boiler room):* Ma! Yuh hear me?

Ma Fishyer: Yess, Pa! *(To* MISS PAGE.) Yuh *vill* take care off her?

Fishyer: Ma! Come here!

Ma Fishyer *(she chokes back the tears as she opens the door to the boiler room):* Yess, Pa, I em c-comin'! *(She whispers back to* MISS PAGE.) And pleese, alvays to remember—Pa should know nodding agenst her. *(She backs out, murmuring.)* No-nodding—n-n-odding.

(MISS PAGE *dries her own tears and looks about the room with distaste. Then she goes resolutely to the door and opens it.)*

Miss Page *(calling softly):* Annie! Annie! *(Motions.)* Come out here! (MISS PAGE *walks to table.)*

(ANNIE *enters and closes door softly. She listens attentively, her face pressed against the door.)*

Miss Page *(back of* EMIL'S *chair):* What have you been telling them?

Annie *(on the defensive):* Nuthin' much—only that I worked for ya as a hired girl!

Miss Page: Why did you do that?

Annie *(back of armchair):* So's to get away from here! If he thought I wuz a dishwasher in a restaurant I'd hafta live here! *(She shudders.)* Nuthin' doin'! I had seventeen years of it!

Miss Page: Yes, but still this is your home.

Annie: Yeh! *(Tremulously.)* And I know what it's like!

Miss Page: Didn't you tell anyone? (ANNIE *shakes her head.)* Not even your mother?

Annie *(goes quickly toward* MISS PAGE; *aghast):* And have him beat it outta her? Whadda ya think I am?

Miss Page *(puzzled):* Why did you tell them you worked for me?

Annie: Well, I—I hadda give somebody's name and yuh wuz de only one I could think of! *(Glances quickly toward closed door, then pleads.)* B-before that happened last year, Miss Page, I n-nearly w-went crazy, and when I fell over *that time* and ya sent m-me to de home until e-everything wuz over—I—j-jest sorta never forgotcha!

Miss Page *(severely):* Yes, but what has that to do with all this?

Annie: W-well, I n-needed some sorta alibi fer stayin' away from here *(moves slowly away)* s-so I—I told 'em I *worked* for ya and that ya wuz goin' out to de *c-country* and I hadda go 'long!

Miss Page *(insistent):* And what else?

Annie: W-well, when I got outta de *hospital,* I stuck to my story and only came here Thursdays.

Miss Page *(with a helpless gesture):* Oh, Annie, why can't you behave yourself?

Annie *(vehemently):* I *do,* Miss Page, honest I do! *(Moves away to escape* MISS PAGE'S *searching eyes.)* B-but I can't help it if there's a-always somebody s-snitchin' on ya!

Miss Page *(reproachfully):* Snitching! But Annie—

Annie *(nervously, twisting and untwisting her belt):* I d-don't care *what* they say! I—I didn't pick up with that feller on de s-street! He—h-he wuz in de room when I g-got in last night!

Miss Page *(coming toward her, slowly):* And *how* did he get there?

Annie *(feebly):* Oh—er—one of de girls musta let'm have de key!

Miss Page *(sadly):* Those girls! (ANNIE *shrinks farther away.)* Why do you live with them? You promised me the last time you wouldn't have anything more to do with Mame and Lottie!

Annie *(haltingly):* But they'se so good to me, Mis' Page! I gotta live someplace—it might as well be with dem—

Miss Page: . . . and get yourself constantly into trouble?

Annie *(protesting):* Oh, Miss Page! Ya don't want me to live *here,* do ya? *(Tremulously.)* Gee, if it wuzn't fer Ma I'd n-never come h-here! B-but Ma *(her whole heart is in her voice)* she's m-my M-ma *(sobs)* s-she's m-my M-m-ma!

Miss Page *(walks up and puts her arm around* ANNIE'S *shaking shoulders, holds her tight):* What's going to become of you, Annie?

Annie *(with hopeless shrug):* I dunno—and I don't care! *(Moves away.)* Just so long *(nods to door)* as *he* don't ketch on!

Miss Page *(walks thoughtfully back a few steps toward door before turning):* Do you know why I came here tonight?

Annie: N-no.

Miss Page: I came here to find out the kind of home you have, so when I see the judge (ANNIE *looks up, startled)* tomorrow morning, I can tell him a little more about you!

Annie *(whispers):* A-about me?

Miss Page: Yes! *(Earnestly.)* I've always been on the square with you, haven't I, Annie? (ANNIE *nods.)* And I want to help you all I can. *But* you've been picked up four times during the last five months for loitering on the streets late at night! *(As* ANNIE *starts to appeal.)* And *last* night the *police* raided the flat you were in!

Annie *(protesting):* But honest, Mis' Page, I couldn't help it! *(She looks about her like a hunted animal.)* Ya see, I wuz-wuz-shhh!

(The areaway door has opened and MRS. FLOYD *appears on top stair.)*

Mrs. Floyd *(her beady eyes glisten in anticipation as she surveys* ANNIE): Hello, there! *(She stumps down the stairs.)*

Annie *(instinctively on the defensive):* H-hello! *(Moves forward to head her off.)* Ma's helping Pa!

(MISS PAGE *crosses to sofa.)*

Mrs. Floyd *(shaking off* ANNIE'S *restraining hand):* Oh, is she now! *(Pulls out* EMIL'S *chair.)* Then I'll wait fer her!

Annie *(in desperate fear, jerks* MRS. FLOYD *around):* I toldja, she's helpin' Pa!

Mrs. Floyd *(flinging* ANNIE *against the cupboard):* Listen, girlie, I gotcha de *first* time!

(MA FISHYER *enters hastily.)*

Annie *(almost hysterical in her fright):* Then beat it!

Ma Fishyer: Ach, Mis' Floyd, I heard yuh close yur door! Ve–ve heff company now–maybe it be better ve go on to *yer* flet–

Mrs. Floyd: Oh, this suits me, I ain't pertic'ler! *(Seats herself in* EMIL'S *chair. Watching* ANNIE *signaling to* MISS PAGE.) Who's her friend?

Ma Fishyer *(nervously):* Oxcuse me, but dis iss Annie's Mis' Page–

Mrs. Floyd *(in response to* MISS PAGE'S *nod):* Pleased to meetcha! (ANNIE *crosses over to her mother and whispers distractedly in her ear.)*

Ma Fishyer: Ve ain't finished our supper yet! Maybe it's better I come ofer and see yuh efter vile.

Mrs. Floyd *(not to be budged):* After while nuthin'! What did she say?

(PA FISHYER *enters unnoticed, wiping his hands.)*

Ma Fishyer *(piteously):* Pleese, Mis' Floyd, eny minute now–Pa–Pa comes–

Mrs. Floyd *(she thumbs toward* ANNIE): Did she say she wuz arrested?

Fishyer: Arrested! *(All look up in surprise.* ANNIE *cowers against the sink.)* Who vas arrested?

Ma Fishyer *(at bay):* Ach, Mis' Floyd hass just been talkin'–er–no vitch vay to me, h'aintcha, Mis' Floyd?

Fishyer: Na–all right! *(He thunders at his wife.)* But who vas arrested?

Mrs. Floyd: Who? *(Spitefully.)* Well, Mr. Fishyer, a'course it ain't none of *my* business, *but* seeing what good neighbors we been and how *pertic'ler* ya wuz to let me know that my son is a good-fer-nuthin' loafer—I take great pleasure ta letcha know that one of *yer* swell family is, wuz, or will be arrested!

Fishyer: Vat? My family vat I bring up so strict?

Mrs. Floyd *(she cackles derisively):* Uhuh! Ain't it the limit?

Fishyer *(purpling with rage):* Who iss it?

Ma Fishyer *(clinging to his arm):* Pa, pleese—P-Pa—

Fishyer *(he shakes her off):* Na, are yuh deef? Na—*who,* I say?

Mrs. Floyd *(vindictively):* Who else but yer Annie!

(ANNIE *becomes deathly pale and shrinks against the wall.)*

Fishyer *(turns furiously): Vat?*

Ma Fishyer *(thrusts herself between* FISHYER *and* ANNIE, *frantically):* Mis' Page, Mis' Page—

Annie *(clasping her mother convulsively, whimpers):* M-ma!

Miss Page *(quickly):* There—there must be some mistake! Where did you hear this, Mrs. Floyd?

Mrs. Floyd: Well—a friend of mine went ta the Domestic Relations Court today ta see about that husband of her'n—a perfect brute—

Fishyer *(impatiently):* Yeh, nefer mind about de brute!

Mrs. Floyd: And so I went along, because I been readin' a dandy story about the Morals Court—yeh know *(she winks to* MISS PAGE *as she thumbs in* ANNIE'S *direction)* where them girls are taken—and so I sez ta myself, sez I—

Fishyer *(exasperated):* Vat?

Mrs. Floyd: That's what I'm comin' ta. So I sez ta myself, I'll visit the Morals Court and see if them fellas from the papers tells the truth! (FISHYER *almost beside himself with frenzy.)* But I stayed so long with my friend that the judge wuz jest closin' fer the day. *But* who should I see there—but Annie!

Fishyer *(choking with wrath, turns wildly with uplifted fist toward* ANNIE): Annie, come here!

Ma Fishyer *(holding him back):* Don't, Pa, pleese, don't—

Fishyer *(trying to loosen her hold):* Keep quiet!

Miss Page *(resolutely):* That isn't anything at all, Mr. Fishyer!

Fishyer *(bellows):* Vat *more* yuh vant, efter bringin' up a girl so strict?

Ma Fishyer *(screams in terror as she feels herself overpowered):* Pa, pleese, P-pa—

Fishyer: Vill yuh keep quiet! *(Furiously to* ANNIE, *whimpering in terror.)* First, I giff yuh someding to remember me by—and den out off de *house* yuh go!

Ma Fishyer *(fighting to hold him back):* N-no, Pa, don't—

Fishyer *(throwing her on the floor in front of table):* Get out off my vay, Ma! *(He shouts, enraged.)* Annie, come here! Yuh hear me! *(He grasps her left arm and jerks her toward him.)*

Annie *(writhing in pain as he tightens his hold):* No—no! It's—it's a lie—a lie—

Mrs. Floyd *(rising in surprise):* Huh!

Annie: Yes, it is! *(She glares about her with the desperation of a trapped animal.)* Yes, it is! I—I wuz—there *(she points sobbingly to* MISS PAGE) with her!

Fishyer: Mit her? Mis' Page?

Annie *(trying to loosen his grip):* Yes, I wuz helpin' her carry her books *(she nods to* MRS. FLOYD) when she musta seen me!

(MISS PAGE *is startled at* ANNIE'S *lie.)*

Fishyer *(tightening his cruel hold until she falls sobbing on her knees):* Vat yuh mean?

Annie *(the words fairly tumble from her twitching lips):*

Mis' Page works fer de judge—h-helps him— And I often go to de court with h-her, don't I, Mis' Page?

(An agonizing second. MISS PAGE *gives one glance at* MA FISHYER'S *prostrated form on the floor and then rises to the occasion.)*

Miss Page: Yes! She's *always* there with me!

Annie *(sobs):* And—I been there lots of times, ain't I, Mis' Page?

(Quickly, before MISS PAGE *can reply,* MA FISHYER *thrusts herself between* PA FISHYER *and* ANNIE.)

Ma Fishyer *(tries to separate his iron grip from* ANNIE'S *arm):* Yuh see, Pa? Yuh see?

Fishyer *(to* MISS PAGE, *slightly mollified):* Ef she's vid *yuh,* Mis'—dot's all right, den! *(Flings* ANNIE *and* MA FISHYER *from him. While* MA FISHYER *tenderly kisses* ANNIE'S *arm he turns wrathfully toward* MRS. FLOYD.) *But!* (MRS. FLOYD, *seeing his intentions, scurries up the stairs.)* Good-by, Mis' Floyd! *(Runs up the stairs and shouts after her.)* And next time yuh *look* first before yuh jump! *(Crashes door after her.)*

(MA FISHYER *is holding* ANNIE *tightly in her arms. Both are weeping.)*

Fishyer: So! *(Comes down stairs.)* Dis should be a lesson for yuh, Annie! Yuh see now vat maybe heppens ef I don't bring yuh up so strict! *(Shakes fist after* MRS. FLOYD.) Dat cat vat just left might be in de right!

(EMIL *re-enters and moves wonderingly toward sink.)*

Ma Fishyer *(her breath sobbing in her throat):* Y-yess, Pa, y-yess—

Fishyer *(sternly flinging her away from* ANNIE *so that she falls into* EMIL'S *arms):* Let her alone, Ma! Vat kind off bringin' up is dot? *(To* MISS PAGE.) I tell yuh, mis', my fadder alvays said: "Order rules de vorld, but *man* iss ruled vid de *vhip!*" And he vas right! *(Glares at* ANNIE.) He ruled us vid a hand off iron! *(To* MISS PAGE.) And look on me! I haf de greatest respect for my fadder! *(Gives them all a menacing look.)* And I do de same! Alvays am I strict and ven dey grow old, dey'll tank me for it!

(He sits down at the table and motions EMIL *to his seat again.* EMIL *sidles into his chair guardedly.* PA FISHYER *begins his meal, dipping his chunk of rye bread in the gravy.* MISS PAGE *notices the looks of hatred darted at* PA FISHYER *by both* ANNIE *and* EMIL.)

Miss Page *(curiously):* And–did you love your father, Mr. Fishyer?

Fishyer *(taken aback):* Lofe? *(He stops with his coffee cup halfway.)* Shure, I lofe him ven I respect him! *(Grimly.)* Huh! *(Cracking an imaginary whip.)* He'd make us dance to de muzik off de stick ef ve didn't lofe him! Shure *(he pauses)*, shure, de children alvays lofe *(fixes his eye on* EMIL, *who immediately stops drinking his coffee)* de *fadder!*

(EMIL *draws back in consternation.)*

Miss Page *(seeing the futility of the situation, turns thoughtfully to the sofa for her gloves and purse):* Well, it's late and I must be going! *(She pauses a second in thought, then comes to a decision.)* By the way, Mr. Fishyer, would you mind if I take Annie with me?

Fishyer: Right avay? I vanted to giff her a good talkin' to, yet!

Miss Page *(pulling on her gloves):* I'm so sorry, but I'm leaving for the country early in the morning–

Ma Fishyer *(staring fixedly at* MISS PAGE): De c-country?

Miss Page *(smiling at her, very gently):* The *real* country, Mrs. Fishyer!

Fishyer *(he grunts, between mouthfuls):* Shure, mit yuh it's all right! *(Over his shoulder to* ANNIE.) Put on yur tings, Annie!

(For a moment, while his back is turned, MA FISHYER *crushes* ANNIE *sobbingly to her breast, kissing her again and again.)*

Annie *(covering her mother's tear-stained cheeks with kisses, she whispers brokenly):* Don't, Ma, don't, I'll be good! I'll be good!

Ma Fishyer *(sobs, clinging to her):* Annie– (MISS PAGE, *separating the two, holds* MA FISHYER *tight in her arms.)* Little Annie!

Miss Page *(while* ANNIE *gets her coat and hat from the coat rack):* Good-by, Mrs. Fishyer. You needn't worry! *(Looks sternly at* PA FISHYER, *unconcernedly eating his meal.)* I'll take good care of your Annie!

(MA FISHYER, *unable to utter a word, leans over and kisses* MISS PAGE'S *hand.* MISS PAGE *turns and mounts the stairs leading to the areaway. As she opens the door,* FISHYER *looks up.)*

Fishyer: Good-by, mis', and ef she don't behave herself (ANNIE *clings to* MISS PAGE; *he balls his fist)* yuh just let me know!

Miss Page *(her arm protectingly around* ANNIE, *she eyes him, half sadly, half ironically):* Yes, indeed! You'd be a *great* help!

Fishyer *(nods his self-satisfaction and takes his second cupful of coffee):* Shure!

(MA FISHYER *leans heavily against* EMIL'S *chair, her eyes following the two disappearing through the doorway.)*

"Copies of this play, in individual paper covered acting editions, are available from Samuel French, Inc., 25 W. 45th St., New York, N. Y. or 7623 Sunset Blvd., Hollywood, Calif. or in Canada Samuel French, (Canada) Ltd., 26 Grenville St., Toronto, Canada."

The Whipping

The old woman across the way
   is whipping the boy again
and shouting to the neighborhood
   her goodness and his wrongs.

Wildly he crashes through elephant ears,
   pleads in dusty zinnias,
while she in spite of crippling fat
   pursues and corners him.

She strikes and strikes the shrilly circling
   boy till the stick breaks
in her hand. His tears are rainy weather
   to woundlike memories:

My head gripped in bony vise
   of knees, the writhing struggle
to wrench free, the blows, the fear
   worse than blows that hateful

Words could bring, the face that I
   no longer knew or loved . . .
Well, it is over now, it is over,
   and the boy sobs in his room,

And the woman leans muttering against
   a tree, exhausted, purged—
avenged in part for lifelong hidings
   she has had to bear.

Robert Hayden

Why does she beat the boy?

Where do the speaker's sympathies lie?

How do *you* sometimes "purge" or "avenge" yourself?

Are you proud of it?

My Papa's Waltz

The whiskey on your breath
Could make a small boy dizzy;
But I hung on like death:
Such waltzing was not easy.

He romped until the pans
Slid from the kitchen shelf;
My mother's countenance
Could not unfrown itself.

The hand that held my wrist
Was battered on one knuckle;
At every step you missed
My right ear scraped a buckle.

You beat time on my head
With a palm caked hard by dirt,
Then waltzed me off to bed
Still clinging to your shirt.

Theodore Roethke

Hannah Armstrong

I wrote him a letter asking him for old times' sake
To discharge my sick boy from the army;
But maybe he couldn't read it.
Then I went to town and had James Garber,
Who wrote beautifully, write him a letter;
But maybe that was lost in the mails.
So I traveled all the way to Washington.
I was more than an hour finding the White House.
And when I found it they turned me away,
Hiding their smiles. Then I thought:
"Oh, well, he ain't the same as when I boarded him
And he and my husband worked together
And all of us called him Abe, there in Menard."
As a last attempt I turned to a guard and said:
"Please say it's old Aunt Hannah Armstrong
From Illinois, come to see him about her sick boy
In the army."
Well, just in a moment they let me in!
And when he saw me he broke in a laugh,
And dropped his business as president,
And wrote in his own hand Doug's discharge,
Talking the while of the early days,
And telling stories.

Edgar Lee Masters

Everybody's had experience with "red tape." How does it get in the way of people caring about each other?

Pick of the Season

Warren Halliburton

Throwing up his hands was Mr. Vasquez' way of ending the discussion. There was nothing more to argue with his son. The matter was over, finished. If Fernando was not willing to work any further in the orchards picking apples, then he could leave the family and take off as his own man. At sixteen he would learn how hard the world was outside. "You are nothing," he had explained to his son in the peculiar kind of way he had of talking. "What is this school?" It was not a question. Mr. Vasquez knew. School was a crazy place for a boy half Indian, half Mexican. Such a boy picked the crop as his family did, and all the other families that Vasquez knew. It was the way of his people to keep from starving because there was nothing else for them.

"It is where I want to go," Fernando said as if that were an answer, especially for a son to give such a man as Mr. Vasquez.

It was late in the season for apples. There was not much time before they would spoil. Many of the families had already left the migrant camp for work elsewhere. The Vasquezes had remained on with other families. There were still apples to fill bushels. And the more bushels filled, the more money earned. With eleven mouths to feed, Mr. Vasquez needed all the money he could earn.

They had worked hard all through the summer, picking crops. From the citrus fruits of the South the family had traveled with other migrant workers until they had worked their way up into the North. Fernando had worked hard, harder than his father had ever seen the boy work. But, then, Fernando was growing into a man.

And men worked harder than boys. Mr. Vasquez was proud of his oldest son.

"You let him go," Mrs. Vasquez said. She had not said anything all through the talk of her men. Now she spoke. Mr. Vasquez looked at his wife and saw that the business about school was not over, finished, as he had thought. He threw up his hands again, this time with different meaning. He was giving in to Fernando. It was such a crazy thing, this idea the boy had about school.

Fernando did not know when nor why he had wanted to go. He had seen many schools the months his family moved about picking the different crops. In all his life he had been inside very few schools and only for short periods of time. Migrant workers always had to move to where there was another crop to earn money. It was a way of life. But it was no way to learn. Fernando understood this. All the time he worked he thought about

what he had learned in the schools. The different things the teachers talked about were like the miracle of the crops. The way they were born from the soil to grow so beautiful was good.

Fernando knew school had started because of the yellow bus that ran past the shacks where the migrant workers lived. It was filled with young people. They shouted at Fernando and his family. Fernando never knew what they said. He knew only that they were happy and that he wanted to join them. It would be only for a little while, but he would learn some more. His family did not have much more to pick. Most of the apples had fallen from the trees. Even the smallest of his brothers and sisters could help fill the bushels.

The walk to the central school house was three miles. His mother had kissed Fernando good-bye; his father did not stop picking up the apples. Fernando understood and went away feeling that his father had kissed him too. The countryside was quiet and beautiful. Everything was turning into different colors. It was such a time to live. Fernando's heart was filled with excitement.

The school house was larger than any Fernando had ever seen. There were few people around. Fernando knew that they were all inside teaching and learning. He knew how to find his way to the office. Inside a lady looked at him. She was not used to him, Fernando could tell. He smiled at her surprise. But she turned away. Fernando waited until another lady came to him. She was wearing a nice smile.

"Can I help you?" she asked. Fernando said that he had come to school. The lady looked funny, the smile no longer on her face. But then she smiled again, a different smile, Fernando thought, although he did not understand. "I see," she said, and hurried away. She returned with a little smiling man. Then she went away.

"I am Mr. Proctor, the principal," the little, smiling man announced and offered his hand. "Perhaps I can help you." Fernando shook the hand and repeated his statement. "I see," Mr. Proctor said and glanced around him. "Well, you look like a big, strapping boy. I guess all that fresh air. You are one of our migrant workers, aren't you?"

Fernando nodded.

Mr. Proctor declared, "You are entitled to attend our school, of course. Although I must confess I haven't the faintest idea how they expect us to do anything about you people without any kind of records or anything else. You're not expected to have all the training of our own youngsters, through no fault of your own. Yet, you're supposed to be able to compete with them on an equal level. It's quite distressing, quite unfair, I must say. You can understand what I'm saying, can't you?"

Fernando shook his head.

The principal registered surprise, and he looked at the boy as if for the first time. "Well, I must admire your honesty."

"I want to go to school," Fernando said.

"And single-mindedness of purpose," Mr. Proctor added, not without a bit of annoyance. He sighed and said, "Well, we'll see what we can do. Perhaps if we can make the school board see what I'm talking about, they'll change a few rules around here. Yes," he agreed with himself, "maybe you'll serve a purpose after all."

Mr. Proctor himself led Fernando into Miss Dalton's classroom. The youngster felt different the instant he entered the room. In place of the dream was the reality of teacher and students. They had all stopped to stare at him. He felt suddenly out of place. It was not that he was in any way ashamed. Fernando had worked hard to come to school scrubbed, his clothes spotless, although wrinkled. But some of the clothes of the students were wrinkled, too. It was something else that made him feel ill at ease. He tried to ward off the feeling, determined as he was to make a success of his school experience.

Fernando nodded his head as he heard the principal introducing him to Miss Dalton. "He's from one of our little migrant camps." Then he listened to the teacher as she introduced him to the class and heard the boys and girls snicker. It was the same way his younger brothers and sisters acted when they were embarrassed. Fernando looked up and smiled.

"Fernando," the teacher announced in a shrill voice, "will take the seat next to Julius Roland. Julius, will you raise your hand?" Julius waved his hand lazily. The class giggled. Miss Dalton silenced them with a reading assignment and a warning. "I have to step out into the hall with Mr. Proctor for a moment. I expect that you will be prepared," she insisted over the softly suggestive whistles of the students, "for any question I might have on the lesson. Fernando, you might look on with Julius until I have time to give you a book of your own."

Fernando smiled at the sea of faces around him. Then he looked at Julius and his book. Julius shoved the book in Fernando's direction. It was upside-down. Fernando studied the letters, then looked up. "The book is upside-down," he said, a little embarrassed.

Julius was looking ahead, a sober expression on his face. He turned and faced Fernando. "What difference does it make?" he asked.

The class burst into laughter. And, just as quickly they stopped. It was as though they did not want to miss anything that was going to happen.

"I cannot read upside-down."

Julius appeared genuinely surprised. "Oh, that's too

bad. All of us learned to read that way. It's much faster once you get onto it."

Fernando eyed the boy, then smiled. "You are funny," he said.

"*I'm* funny!" Julius looked suddenly indignant.

The class broke up laughing.

"Ask him if he can read right side up," a girl called out from the front of the room.

Julius seemed taken with the idea. "Can you read at all?" he demanded.

Fernando nodded his head. "But I should like to read better. That is why I have come to school."

"Ask him," a boy called out from across the room but was immediately interrupted.

"Ask him yourself," Julius said.

The boy laughed. "Which would you rather do, read or pick apples?"

"I have to pick the apples. I like to read. It is why I am here," Fernando explained.

"Which can you do better?"

Fernando looked ahead at the girl and slowly shook his head. "I do not understand."

"Pick apples or read," another boy explained.

Fernando smiled thoughtfully. The class waited as if disbelieving that this strange boy could be seriously considering the question. "I think maybe I pick the apples better. It is because of the practice."

As if mocking his seriousness, the class nodded at the logic of the statement. Some suppressed giggles.

"But maybe I should begin my practice in reading," he suggested to Julius. The boy slowly turned the book right side up and shoved it at Fernando. The class watched, waiting to enjoy more of the newcomer. "You are not reading?" Fernando asked.

"No, I am not reading," Julius answered mockingly.

Fernando looked at the boy, unable to understand his anger. Then he decided to look at the book and study the strange map drawn at the top of the page.

Disappointed that he should desert them for the reading assignment, the class grew restless. Some sighed and slouched over their own readers. Others were not so easily put off. "Don't worry," one of them announced, "he's only looking at the picture." Another student took up the idea. "That's how he knew the book was upside-down. You got to learn *something* picking all them apples!" The remark brought the laughter of the class as Miss Dalton stormed back into the room.

"It doesn't sound as though there's much study going on in here," she charged. She sent a withering look around the class. The students plunged into their books. Spotting Fernando, Miss Dalton remarked, "Well, it doesn't seem to have taken you long to catch on to our sneaky little ways."

Fernando did not respond; his interest was absorbed by the page.

The teacher grew incensed. "Oh," she exclaimed, "and I'm to have insolence besides!"

Sensing that something had changed around him, Fernando looked up. He saw the teacher and smiled.

"Well," she remarked, trying to match his expression with a grin of her own, "we certainly look pleased enough with ourselves. Perhaps you wouldn't mind telling us all about what you were supposed to be reading." The students knew the suggestion to be a command.

"Yes, ma'am," Fernando answered, then hesitated.

"Well, go on, unless there's something bothering you!"

Fernando shook his head. "It's about calling the United States, America."

"Yes, go on."

"The book, it describes our country as if it was America." The youngster frowned, seeing that no one was understanding what he was explaining. "But there is South America, too."

Miss Dalton said, "I'm afraid you'll have to do better than that."

"The United States, it is only part of America."

The class started to laugh. Miss Dalton silenced them with a look. "Yes, there is South America. But that hardly seems important, does it?"

Fernando looked up, his expression questioning what the teacher had said.

Miss Dalton immediately realized what she had said and decided against pursuing the issue. She was satisfied that the boy had at least been reading the book. It was more than she expected from the class. She decided to change the subject.

"But, perhaps, you would want to tell us something about yourself. We've never had a member from any of our migrant camps in our school. It is an opportunity for us to learn something about you people, how you live and different places you go to."

Fernando seemed pleased. "You would want to know these things?" he asked disbelievingly. Then he saw that they were all looking interested. "It is sometimes not the good life. I feel that you should know this. At times it is very hard. There is not much money. And when the crop is poor, there is no money. But it is not always bad. You will see," he said brightening. "You will come visit with us!"

The Vasquez family was not nearly so taken with the idea of Fernando's invitation. "You want they should laugh?" Mr. Vasquez said waving his hand around the ramshackle room of their cabin. Mrs. Vasquez simply held her head. The children were all excited over the idea and had to be chased outside. Fernando could not understand. "This is where we live," he declared and looked proudly around him. "It is good. They will see."

Mrs. Vasquez continued to wag her head at the terrible thought.

"We have a week to clean up nice," Fernando said hopefully.

"Perhaps, by that time, we will be gone," Mr. Vasquez comforted his wife.

The rest of his school week Fernando tried to understand the ways of his classmates. They were very playful, he thought. He could not understand why he had become such a favorite in so short a time. The questions Fernando asked in class made some of his teachers angry. The students were amused. In math he wanted to know how the logarithm table was figured out; in English he questioned rules that had nothing to do with the clarity of the sentence; the same way in foreign language, where half the class was divided into French, the other Spanish. He asked why they should learn how to write before they could speak the language.

But it was in earth science that Fernando scored the most, and against Miss Dalton. "Hey, Fernando," the students called out, "you sure told old prune face today!" Miss Dalton had remarked that deserts were dry wastelands without food or life. Fernando apologized but pointed out that both were there, citing the cactus for starters. Another time Fernando could not understand why Miss Dalton would call the early American Indian a savage. He explained what he knew of Indian culture. Miss Dalton tried dismissing such primitive relics and lore, but the class was interested because the Indians had suddenly become people.

It appeared as if everywhere Miss Dalton turned Fernando was there with information. One was about the produce of the region. Fernando explained how, many years ago, potatoes were grown where there are now apple orchards. "The soil has to grow different crops. Otherwise it will go bad." Miss Dalton suffered the boy's lectures. She had learned to hold her reaction down. "I see," was all she said when finally he finished. What she saw was the boy's insolence.

When she explained how weather changes took care of the crops so that they would grow strong and healthy, Fernando offered examples of how some weather changes destroyed crops. Then the lesson came alive.

As the week progressed the attitude of the youngsters shifted. Instead of baiting Fernando out of boredom, they waited for him and listened to him. They grew loyal to what he had to say and started to distrust their teachers, especially those who they knew disliked Fernando. Miss Dalton became their favorite target. "Why, she's been teaching us a whole bunch of junk and we didn't even know it."

"Not until Fernando came," a female admirer added.

Fernando would hear none of it. "I know only the little things," he said. "Miss Dalton, she knows all the big things."

Miss Dalton's lesson had gone poorly. She told herself that, after all, it was Friday, that the students were distracted. But she knew better. It was because of Fernando. Throughout the lesson he had not volunteered once. The fact that her lesson had in one miserable week become dependent upon this boy was insulting. "Fernando," she snapped, "since we have not heard from you all period, I think you should tell us a little about our visit to your home next week."

Something was disturbing the boy. For answer

Fernando simply shook his head, a sad expression on his face. He looked at his classmates and saw that all were watching him. Some smiled, and others nodded. Fernando felt encouraged. "It is where we live," he shrugged. Then he slowly, almost as though talking to himself, began explaining how it was to travel the country and not be a part of it. He described the beauty of the land and the pain because it was not yours. Because you could never remain. He described how people were always strangers to him. "The same way, I guess, they feel we are strangers." And he smiled a wan smile.

"But always it is the work. Even at night the work is still in your bones. Especially the bones of the older ones. I see my mother and my father, and they are tired. The children they have gone to bed. My parents tell me to go to bed. They are sad in a way they do not want me to see. They think maybe I am still a baby. They do not know that I too am sad. It is such a life, living from one place to another place. It is no good for to learn." And he lifted his book and shook it. "That is why I come to school. It is good," he said and looked around at the class of boys and girls.

When he finished no one spoke, not even Miss Dalton. She tried getting back to the lesson, but no one was surprised when she simply gave them free reading time.

The class no longer looked forward to visiting the camp where Fernando lived. They knew enough about conditions at migrant camps to realize what they had been up to. They were shocked and embarrassed. Fernando was their friend. And to visit the miserable camp was no way to expose a friend. They dreaded the Monday trip, yet knew that somehow it was their responsibility to attend, to show Fernando that they were his friends.

The bus trip from school to camp was made in

silence. No one bothered to look up as the bus approached the dusty road winding onto the camp grounds. Some wondered about Fernando, why he was nowhere about to greet them. A few stole questioning looks at one another. Not until they spilled out onto the grounds did the students realize that the Vasquez family had left. Fernando had known on Friday. It was why he had been so sad.

They drew a sigh of relief.

The feeling was short-lived. Fernando was gone, and they would not see him again. But then they looked around them at the shacks and naked vineyards. Suddenly they saw it as Fernando had explained the life of a migrant worker in class. And they understood things they had never realized before. Fernando had come to school to learn, but he had taught them so much more. And they were grateful for the opportunity of making friends with the half-frightened families who had stood staring. The boys and girls wanted them to know that they were welcomed before they too would be leaving for another camp.

What details in the story invite you to accept Fernando as a *person,* and not just as a migrant worker's son?

Have you ever considered putting yourself on the line for a place to sit?

The Bench

Richard Rive

"We form an integral part of a complex society, a society in which a vast proportion of the population is denied the very basic right of existence, a society that condemns a man to an inferior position because he has the misfortune to be born black, a society that can only retain its precarious social and economic position at the expense of an enormous oppressed mass!"

The speaker paused for a moment and sipped some water from a glass. Karlie's eyes shone as he listened. Those were great words, he thought, great words and true. Karlie sweated. The hot November sun beat down on the gathering. The trees on the Grand Parade in Johannesburg afforded very little shelter, and his handkerchief was already soaked where he had placed it between his neck and his shirt collar. Karlie stared around him at the sea of faces. Every shade of color was represented, from shiny ebony to the one or two whites in the crowd. Karlie stared at the two detectives who were busily making shorthand notes of the speeches, then turned to stare back at the speaker.

"It is up to us to challenge the right of any group who willfully and deliberately condemn a fellow group to a servile position. We must challenge the right of any people who see fit to segregate human beings solely on grounds of pigmentation. Your children are denied the rights which are theirs by birth. They are segregated educationally, socially, economically. . . ."

Ah, thought Karlie, that man knows what he is speaking about. He says I am as good as any other man, even a white man. That needs much thinking. I wonder if he means I have the right to go to any bioscope, or eat in any restaurant, or that my children can go to a white school. These are dangerous ideas and need much thinking. I wonder what Ou Klaas would say to this. Ou Klaas said that God made the white man and the black man separately, and the one must always be "baas" and the other "jong." But this man says different things and somehow they ring true.

Karlie's brow was knitted as he thought. On the platform were many speakers, both white and black, and they were behaving as if there were no differences of color among them. There was a white woman in a blue dress offering Nxeli a cigarette. That never could have happened at Bietjiesvlei. Old Lategan at the store there would have fainted if his Annatjie had offered Witbooi a cigarette. And Annatjie wore no such pretty dress.

These were new things and he, Karlie, had to be careful before he accepted them. But why shouldn't he accept them? He was not a Colored man any more; he was a human being. The last speaker had said so. He remembered seeing pictures in the newspapers of people who defied laws which relegated them to a particular class, and those people were smiling as they went to prison. This was a queer world.

The speaker continued and Karlie listened intently. He spoke slowly, and his speech was obviously carefully prepared. This is a great man, thought Karlie.

The last speaker was the white lady in the blue dress, who asked them to challenge any discriminatory laws or measures in their own way. Why should she speak like that? She could go to the best bioscopes and swim at

the best beaches. Why, she was even more beautiful than Annatjie Lategan.

They had warned him in Bietjiesvlei about coming to the city. He had seen the skollies in District Six and he knew what to expect there. Hanover Street held no terrors for him. But no one had told him about this. This was new; this set one's mind thinking; yet he felt it was true. She had said one should challenge. He, Karlie, would astound old Lategan and Van Wyk at the dairy farm. They could do what they liked to him after that. He would smile like those people in the newspapers.

The meeting was almost over when Karlie threaded his way through the crowd. The words of the speakers were still milling through his head. It could never happen in Bietjiesvlei. Or could it? The sudden screech of a car pulling to a stop whirled him back to his senses. A white head was thrust angrily through the window.

"Look where you're going, you black idiot!"

Karlie stared dazedly at him. Surely this white man never heard what the speakers had said. He could never have seen the white woman offering Nxeli a cigarette. He could never imagine the white lady shouting those words at him. It would be best to catch a train and think these things over.

He saw the station in a new light. Here was a mass of human beings, black, white and some brown like himself. Here they mixed with one another, yet each mistrusted the other with an unnatural fear, each treated the other with suspicion, moved in a narrow, haunted pattern of its own. One must challenge these things the speaker had said . . . in one's own way. Yet how in one's own way? How was one to challenge? Suddenly it dawned upon him. Here was his challenge! *The bench.* The railway bench with "Europeans Only" neatly painted on it in white. For one moment it symbolized all the misery of the plural South African society.

Here was a challenge to his rights as a man. Here it stood. A perfectly ordinary wooden railway bench, like thousands of others in South Africa. His challenge. That bench now had concentrated in it all the evils of a system he could not understand and he felt a victim of. It was the obstacle between himself and humanity. If he sat on it, he was a man. If he was afraid, he denied himself membership as a human being in a human society. He almost had visions of righting this pernicious system, if he only sat down on that bench. Here was his chance. He, Karlie, would challenge.

He seemed perfectly calm when he sat down on the bench, but inside his heart was thumping wildly. Two conflicting ideas now throbbed through him. The one said, "I have no right to sit on this bench." The other was the voice of a new religion and said, "Why have I no right to sit on this bench?" The one voice spoke of the past, of the servile position he had occupied on the farm, of his father and his father's father who were born black, lived like blacks, and died like mules. The other voice spoke of new horizons and said, "Karlie, you are a man. You have dared what your father and your father's father would not have dared. You will die like a man."

Karlie took out a cigarette and smoked. Nobody seemed to notice his sitting there. This was an anticlimax. The world still pursued its monotonous way. No voice had shouted, "Karlie has conquered!" He was a normal human being sitting on a bench in a busy station, smoking a cigarette. Or was this his victory: the fact that he was a normal human being?

A well-dressed white woman walked down the platform. Would she sit on the bench? Karlie wondered.

And then that gnawing voice, "You should stand and let the white woman sit!" Karlie narrowed his eyes and gripped tighter at his cigarette. She swept past him without the slightest twitch of an eyelid and continued walking down the platform. Was she afraid to challenge—to challenge his right to be a human being?

Karlie now felt tired. A third conflicting idea was now creeping in, a compensatory idea which said, "You sit on this bench because you are tired; you are tired therefore you sit." He would not move because he was tired, or was it because he wanted to sit where he liked?

People were now pouring out of a train that had pulled into the station. There were so many people pushing and jostling one another that nobody noticed him. This was his train. It would be easy to step into the train and ride off home, but that would be giving in, suffering defeat, refusing the challenge, in fact, admitting that he was not a human being. He sat on. Lazily he blew the cigarette smoke into the air, thinking. . . . His mind was away from the meeting and the bench: he was thinking of Bietjiesvlei and Ou Klaas, how he had insisted that Karlie should come to Cape Town. Ou Klaas would suck on his pipe and look so quizzically at one. He was wise and knew much. He had said one must go to Cape Town and learn the ways of the world. He would spit and wink slyly when he spoke of District Six and the women he knew in Hanover Street. Ou Klaas knew everything. He said God made us white or black and we must therefore keep our places.

"Get off this seat!"

Karlie did not hear the gruff voice. Ou Klaas would be on the land now waiting for his tot of cheap wine.

"I said get off the bench, you swine!" Karlie suddenly whipped back to reality. For a moment he was going to jump up; then he remembered who he was and why he was sitting there. He suddenly felt very tired. He looked up slowly into a very red face that stared down at him.

"Get up!" it said. "There are benches down there for you."

Karlie looked up and said nothing. He stared into a pair of sharp, gray, cold eyes.

"Can't you hear me speaking to you? You black swine!"

Slowly and deliberately Karlie puffed at the cigarette. This was his test. They both stared at each other, challenged with the eyes, like two boxers, each knowing that they must eventually trade blows yet each afraid to strike first.

"Must I dirty my hands on scum like you?"

Karlie said nothing. To speak would be to break the spell, the supremacy he felt was slowly gaining.

An uneasy silence, then, "I will call a policeman rather than soil my hands on a Hotnot like you. You can't even open up your black jaw when a white man speaks to you."

Karlie saw the weakness. The white man was afraid to take action himself. He, Karlie, had won the first round of the bench dispute.

A crowd had now collected.

"Afrika!" shouted a joker.

Karlie ignored the remark. People were now milling around him, staring at the unusual sight of a black man sitting on a white man's bench. Karlie merely puffed on.

"Look at him. That's the worst of giving these Kaffirs enough rope."

"I can't understand it. They have their own benches!"

"Don't get up! You have every right to sit there!"

"He'll get up when a policeman comes!"

"After all, why shouldn't they sit there?"

"I've said before: I've had a native servant once, and a more impertinent . . . "

Karlie sat and heard nothing. Irresolution had now turned to determination. Under no condition was he going to get up. They could do what they liked.

"So, this is the fellow, eh! Get up there! Can't you read?"

The policeman was towering over him. Karlie could see the crest on his buttons and the wrinkles in his neck.

"What is your name and address? Come on!"

Karlie still maintained his obstinate silence. It took the policeman rather unawares. The crowd was growing every minute.

"You have no right to speak to this man in such a manner!" It was the white lady in the blue dress.

"Mind your own business! I'll ask your help when I need it. It's people like you who make these Kaffirs think they're as good as white men. Get up, you!" The latter remark was addressed to Karlie.

"I insist that you treat him with proper respect."

The policeman turned red.

"This . . . this . . . " He was lost for words.

"Kick up the Hotnot if he won't get up!" shouted a spectator. Rudely a white man laid hands on Karlie.

"Get up, you!" Karlie turned to resist, to cling to the bench, his bench. There was more than one man pulling at him. He hit out wildly and then felt a dull pain as somebody rammed a fist into his face. He was bleeding now and wild-eyed. He would fight for it. The constable clapped a pair of handcuffs on him and tried to clear a way through the crowd. Karlie still struggled. A blow or two landed on him. Suddenly he relaxed and slowly struggled to his feet. It was useless to fight any longer. Now it was his turn to smile. He had challenged and won. Who cared the rest? "Come on, you swine!" said the policeman forcing Karlie through the crowd.

"Certainly!" said Karlie for the first time. And he stared at the policeman with all the arrogance of one who dared sit on a "European bench."

Do you admire Karlie for his courage? Despise him for his foolishness? Sympathize with him but disagree with his tactics?

Under what circumstances, if at all, would you take a personal stand when it meant that you had to break a law?

After You, My Dear Alphonse

Shirley Jackson

Mrs. Wilson was just taking the gingerbread out of the oven when she heard Johnny outside talking to someone.

"Johnny," she called, "you're late. Come in and get your lunch."

"Just a minute, Mother," Johnny said. "After you, my dear Alphonse."

"After *you,* my dear Alphonse," another voice said.

"No, after *you,* my dear Alphonse," Johnny said.

Mrs. Wilson opened the door. "Johnny," she said, "you come in this minute and get your lunch. You can play after you've eaten."

Johnny came in after her, slowly. "Mother," he said, "I brought Boyd home for lunch with me."

"Boyd?" Mrs. Wilson thought for a moment. "I don't

believe I've met Boyd. Bring him in, dear, since you've invited him. Lunch is ready."

"Boyd!" Johnny yelled. "Hey, Boyd, come on in!"

"I'm coming. Just got to unload this stuff."

"Well, hurry, or my mother'll be sore."

"Johnny, that's not very polite to either your friend or your mother," Mrs. Wilson said. "Come sit down, Boyd."

As she turned to show Boyd where to sit, she saw he was a Negro boy, smaller than Johnny but about the same age. His arms were loaded with split kindling wood. "Where'll I put this stuff, Johnny?" he asked.

Mrs. Wilson turned to Johnny. "Johnny," she said, "what did you make Boyd do? What is that wood?"

"Dead Japanese," Johnny said mildly. "We stand them in the ground and run over them with tanks."

"How do you do, Mrs. Wilson?" Boyd said.

"How do you do, Boyd? You shouldn't let Johnny make you carry all that wood. Sit down now and eat lunch, both of you."

"Why shouldn't he carry the wood, Mother? It's his wood. We got it at his place."

"Johnny," Mrs. Wilson said, "go on and eat your lunch."

"Sure," Johnny said. He held out the dish of scrambled eggs to Boyd. "After you, my dear Alphonse."

"After *you,* my dear Alphonse," Boyd said.

"After *you,* my dear Alphonse," Johnny said. They began to giggle.

"Are you hungry, Boyd?" Mrs. Wilson asked.

"Yes, Mrs. Wilson."

"Well, don't you let Johnny stop you. He always fusses about eating, so you just see that you get a good lunch. There's plenty of food here for you to have all you want."

"Thank you, Mrs. Wilson."

"Come on, Alphonse," Johnny said. He pushed half the scrambled eggs onto Boyd's plate. Boyd watched while Mrs. Wilson put a dish of stewed tomatoes beside his plate.

"Boyd don't eat tomatoes, do you, Boyd?" Johnny said.

"*Doesn't* eat tomatoes, Johnny. And just because you don't like them, don't say that about Boyd. Boyd will eat *anything*.

"Bet he won't," Johnny said, attacking his scrambled eggs.

"Boyd wants to grow up and be a big strong man so he can work hard," Mrs. Wilson said. "I'll bet Boyd's father eats stewed tomatoes."

"My father eats anything he wants to," Boyd said.

"So does mine," Johnny said. "Sometimes he doesn't eat hardly anything. He's a little guy, though. Wouldn't hurt a flea."

"Mine's a little guy too," Boyd said.

"I'll bet he's strong, though," Mrs. Wilson said. She hesitated. "Does he . . . work?"

"Sure," Johnny said. "Boyd's father works in a factory."

"There, you see?" Mrs. Wilson said. "And he certainly has to be strong to do that—all that lifting and carrying at a factory."

"Boyd's father doesn't have to," Johnny said. "He's a foreman."

Mrs. Wilson felt defeated. "What does your mother do, Boyd?"

"My mother?" Boyd was surprised. "She takes care of us kids."

"Oh. She doesn't work, then?"

"Why should she?" Johnny said through a mouthful of eggs. "You don't work."

"You really don't want any stewed tomatoes, Boyd?"

"No, thank you, Mrs. Wilson," Boyd said.

"No, thank you, Mrs. Wilson, no, thank you, Mrs. Wilson, no, thank you, Mrs. Wilson," Johnny said. "Boyd's sister's going to work, though. She's going to be a teacher."

"That's a very fine attitude for her to have, Boyd." Mrs. Wilson restrained an impulse to pat Boyd on the head. "I imagine you're all very proud of her?"

"I guess so," Boyd said.

"What about all your other brothers and sisters? I guess all of you want to make just as much of yourselves as you can."

"There's only me and Jean," Boyd said. "I don't know yet what I want to be when I grow up."

"We're going to be tank drivers, Boyd and me," Johnny said. "Zoom."

Mrs. Wilson caught Boyd's glass of milk as Johnny's napkin ring, suddenly transformed into a tank, plowed heavily across the table.

"Look, Johnny," Boyd said. "Here's a foxhole. I'm shooting at you."

Mrs. Wilson, with the speed born of long experience, took the gingerbread off the shelf and placed it carefully between the tank and the foxhole.

"Now eat as much as you want to, Boyd," she said. "I want to see you get filled up."

"Boyd eats a lot, but not as much as I do," Johnny said. "I'm bigger than he is."

"You're not much bigger," Boyd said. "I can beat you running."

Mrs. Wilson took a deep breath. "Boyd," she said. Both boys turned to her. "Boyd, Johnny has some suits

that are a little too small for him, and a winter coat. It's not new, of course, but there's lots of wear in it still. And I have a few dresses that your mother or sister could probably use. Your mother can make them over into lots of things for all of you, and I'd be very happy to give them to you. Suppose before you leave I make up a big bundle, and then you and Johnny can take it over to your mother right away. . . ." Her voice trailed off as she saw Boyd's puzzled expression.

"But I have plenty of clothes, thank you," he said. "And I don't think my mother knows how to sew very well, and anyway I guess we buy about everything we need. Thank you very much, though."

"We don't have time to carry that old stuff around, Mother," Johnny said. "We got to play tanks with the kids today."

Mrs. Wilson lifted the plate of gingerbread off the table as Boyd was about to take another piece. "There are many little boys like you, Boyd, who would be very grateful for the clothes someone was kind enough to give them."

"Boyd will take them if you want him to, Mother," Johnny said.

"I didn't mean to make you mad, Mrs. Wilson," Boyd said.

"Don't think I'm angry, Boyd. I'm just disappointed in you, that's all. Now let's not say anything more about it."

She began clearing the plates off the table, and Johnny took Boyd's hand and pulled him to the door. "Bye, Mother," Johnny said. Boyd stood for a minute, staring at Mrs. Wilson's back.

"After you, my dear Alphonse," Johnny said, holding the door open.

"Is your mother still mad?" Mrs. Wilson heard Boyd ask in a low voice.

"I don't know," Johnny said. "She's screwy sometimes."

"So's mine," Boyd said. He hesitated. "After *you,* my dear Alphonse.

Stereotypes are certain characteristics we assign to all people of a certain race or city or class. For example, "All criminals have sneaky eyes." How many stereotypes does Mrs. Wilson have? What harm do they do?

Three Who Went Looking for Death

adapted from Geoffrey Chaucer's "Pardoner's Tale" by Elizabeth Wice

Characters

Narrator	Tavern Boy
Tom	Bartender
Humphrey	Old Man
Perkin	Storekeeper

Scene I

Narrator: We are inside a tavern in an old town, many years ago. It is early morning. Three young men, Tom, Perkin, and Humphrey, have been up all night drinking.

Tom *(calling to* TAVERN BOY): Hey, kid! Bring us another round of drinks!

Tavern boy: Coming, sir.

Humphrey: What are you taking your time for? Hurry up.

Perkin: Yeah, hurry up. When my friend asks you for something, you get it—and on the double.

(A bell rings outside.)

Tom: What's that bell?

Humphrey: It's only the church bell, you idiot. Time for you to go say your morning prayers.

(Bell rings again.)

Tom: It's too early for church.

Tavern boy: That sounds like the bell they ring when you're dead and they carry you to the graveyard.

Tom: The kid's right. Hey, kid! Never mind the drinks. Go outside and see whose body they've got.

Tavern boy: Sir, I don't have to ask. Two hours before you came. I heard all about it.

Perkin: All about what?

Tavern boy: He was an old friend of yours. He died very suddenly last night, right in here.

Perkin: In this room?

Tavern boy: Yes. He was lying on his back, dead drunk, on the bench over there. Someone killed him. They say it was a thief called Death.

Humphrey: Death?

Tavern boy: Yes. They say he's been killing a lot of people around here. Before your friend could turn over, this Death stabbed him right through the heart. Then this Death just walked out, without saying a word. If you don't mind a little advice, let me warn you.

Tom: Warn us about what?

Tavern boy: Watch out for an enemy like that. You can never tell when you might run into him. That's what I've been told, anyhow.

Bartender: The boy is right. Just this year, he killed

every single person in a village a mile from here—even the kids.

Tom: Where's this guy from?

Bartender: Maybe he lives somewhere around that village. No one knows. You better watch out.

Tom: Who says he's so bad? I could lick this Death. Hey, you two guys. Let's make a deal.

Humphrey: What kind of a deal?

Tom: We'll kill this double-crossing Death the way he killed our friend. Let's shake on it. Perkin, come over here. You too, Humphrey.

(The three men stand in a circle and each one puts his right hand in the center.)

Tom: Now let's swear on it. We'll get him today.

Humphrey: I swear it.

Tom: I swear it.

Scene II

Narrator: Tom, Perkin, and Humphrey are on the road to the village that the bartender told them about.

Humphrey: I'm tired. How far is this old village?

Tom: Take it easy, fatso. We've only gone half a mile.

Perkin: Look! Someone's coming toward us!

Tom: Take it easy. It's just some old man.

Old man: Hello.

Tom: You old bum, get out of the way.

Humphrey: Yeah, move.

Perkin: Hey, old man, why are you all wrapped up in that long coat? Don't you know it's summer?

Tom: He's so old he should be dead already.

Old man: Do you want to know why I'm still alive?

Tom: Yeah, tell us.

Old man: I've walked halfway around the world. I've been looking for someone who will trade me his youth for my old age. But I can't find a single person who will make the swap. So now I walk all alone, knocking my cane against the ground and asking Mother Earth to let me be buried. All I want is some rest for my old bones. But old Mother Earth, she won't let me die.

Perkin: Is this guy nuts?

Old man: Young men, let me tell you something else. You shouldn't talk that way to someone my age. You should show some respect to older people.

(The OLD MAN *starts to walk away from them.)*

Tom: Aw, shut up. Hey, wait! you don't get away so easily. It sounds as though you're looking for a person called Death.

Perkin: Yeah, I bet you're his spy or something.

Tom: Tell us where he is—or *else!*

Old man: Well, sir, if you want to find this Death, I'll tell you. See that crooked path into those woods?

Perkin: We have eyes.

Old man: Well, I left him there under an oak tree this morning. You'll find him if you take the path. He's not far. And may God protect you.

Scene III

Narrator: The three young men have come to the oak tree. Under it they find a pile of gold coins.

Humphrey: Are my eyes playing tricks on me?

Tom: No, that's real.

Perkin: Beautiful!

Humphrey: Feel it slide through your fingers.

Perkin: Beautiful, beautiful gold. Let's get it out of here.

Tom: We can't carry all of it away in one day.

Perkin: Why not?

Tom: People would think we stole it.

Humphrey: We'd be locked up for good.

Tom: We've got to wait until it's dark before we sneak this gold back. Meanwhile, I've got an idea. Let's draw lots and see who runs back into town to get us some bread and wine.

Perkin: What will we use?

Tom: Here are some sticks. Look, they're all in my hand. We'll all pull. The one who gets the longest stick is the lucky guy who gets the bread and wine.

Perkin: What about the other two?

Tom: They'll stay here and guard the gold. If our plan works, we'll carry it off tonight. Are you ready?

(They each pull a stick out of TOM'S *hand.)*

Perkin: I got the long one.

Tom: Okay, when you go into town, don't breathe a word about the gold.

Perkin: Don't worry. I'll be back in twenty minutes.

Tom: He's gone. Now we've got it made.

Humphrey: What do you mean?

Tom: Don't be an idiot. Here's all this gold that we're supposed to divide up three ways.

Humphrey: Yeah, it's beautiful.

Tom: Why don't just the two of us split it, instead?

Humphrey: What do we say to Perkin when he gets back?

Tom: Are you my buddy, or aren't you?

Humphrey: You can trust me. Now, what's the plan?

Tom: We are two, and he is only one. Two are twice as strong as one—right?

Humphrey: Right.

Tom: When he comes back, we'll wrestle a little—just for fun. When you have him down, I'll knife him before he figures out what kind of a game we're playing. Then the money's ours.

Humphrey: Half for me . . .

Tom: And half for me.

Narrator: Meanwhile, Perkin is headed back to town for the wine and food. Let's follow him.

Perkin *(to himself):* Isn't that just my luck? Why couldn't I have found that gold when I was alone. Then that whole pile could have been mine—all mine.

Narrator: There is a shop in town that sells rat poison. Perkin goes in there.

Storekeeper: What can I do for you, young fellow?

Perkin: Well, sir, I've got this problem with rats. My cellar is full of them. I can't sleep at night they make so much noise.

Storekeeper: You want to get rid of rats?

Perkin: That's right.

Storekeeper *(handing him a little bottle):* Here's what you want. If any living creature swallows a mouthful of this, he'll drop dead on the spot. That's how strong this poison is.

Perkin: I'll take it. Here's your money.

Narrator: Perkin leaves the store. He finds three empty bottles and washes them out. When no one is watching, he pours the rat poison into two of the bottles.

Perkin *(to himself):* Now, these two bottles have poison in them. This third one I'll keep clean for myself. I'm going to be very thirsty tonight after carrying all of that gold.

Narrator: Perkin buys some wine and fills all three bottles with it. Then he hurries back to his friends.

Tom: Hi, Perkin! What took you so long?

Humphrey: Did you get our bread and wine?

Perkin: I sure did. *(He puts the bottles and bread next to a tree.)*

Humphrey: Hey, Tom, how about a little exercise before lunch?

Tom: Sure thing.

Humphrey: Hey, Perkin, I bet I can pin you in six seconds. *(He runs at Perkin and starts wrestling.)*

Perkin: Hey, what is this, you fat clown?

Humphrey: Take this!

(HUMPHREY *pins* PERKIN *down.* TOM *reaches for his knife and stabs* PERKIN. *The body rolls over and lies still.)*

Tom: Good work?

Humphrey: Whew! I need a drink.

Tom: Good idea. We'll both have something to drink before we get to work digging a hole for that body.

(TOM *picks up one of the poisoned wine bottles and takes a long drink.* HUMPHREY *pulls the cork off the other poisoned bottle.)*

Narrator: The poison worked quickly, just as the storekeeper said it would.

We use the expression "drives wedges between them." What drove the wedge here? What else drives wedges between people?

The Two Climbers

Glenn Meeter

They met because they were both looking for something to do on Sunday. He, Peter Vroom, was in Vermont as part of a convention of canned-goods brokers. He liked his fellow brokers well enough, but on Sunday he preferred not to join them. They would spend the day golfing, drinking, playing cards, or "looking for action" in the nearby small towns. Few of them had cars, and none of these, it seemed, wanted to drive into the village to church, as he would have preferred to do. So when Case found him in front of the inn fireplace on Saturday night, and asked whether he wanted to climb Mt. Jacob, he agreed.

He and Case were alone in front of the fire; the rest of the inn, including most of the brokers, were in the bar, still talking business and filling their lungs with cigarette smoke. It would be good to get away, he thought. Almost like going to church.

Case was a student, very thin, with a bushy blonde mustache. Originally from Holland, he was on his way around the world, "bumming and thumbing." He had heard that the climb to Mt. Jacob was a good hike. Peter had no special love for bearded students, or mustached ones either; he was thirty-seven, and had been out of school for a long time, supporting himself and his family. Students nowadays were more careless and casual about life than he had ever dared to be. Yet something about Case was attractive. Peter's grandparents had come from Holland, before settling in the Midwest, and the way Case talked reminded him of his grandfather. His grandfather had been a very pious man, and he had had a mustache, too.

In the morning Peter was on the inn porch at 9:20. He wore thick-soled hiking boots and wool socks, sweat-shirt, a red wool shirt over that, and grey water-repellent trousers. One shirt pocket held raisins and a candy bar; the other a pair of sunglasses, in case it turned warm, and matches and a scout knife, in case it stormed. In his trouser pockets he had maps of the Mt. Jacob area and his wallet. There was nothing but wilderness around Mt. Jacob, of course, but he couldn't be without his wallet. It held money, credit cards, pictures of his family, his blood type, driver's license—all his identification. He could imagine situations where a rescuer might want to identify him. Around his neck hung his camera and light meter. Next to his chair, as he waited, lay a walking stick he had found near the inn. Good stout oak, as he thought of it, though he had no way of knowing whether it was oak or elm or hickory. He had been up since seven and had had a good breakfast. He had rubbed sunburn lotion, in case the clouds cleared away, into the skin of his nose and around the base of his receding hairline. After waiting five minutes he ran upstairs and came down again with a plastic rain poncho, neatly folded and tied with twine to his belt.

Case appeared at twenty-five to ten. He wore shorts, shirt, and sneakers. No socks. He walked briskly, perhaps to keep off the chill; his mustache was the warmest thing on his skin.

"Well, are we ready?" Peter stood up awkwardly; next to Case he felt heavy, as if he clanked.

"Let me take first breakfast," Case said.

Breakfast was fried egg on bread, from the snack bar. He wolfed it as they walked along. Even on the gravel road he walked jauntily, bouncing on the balls of his feet.

"You won't get cold?"

Case shrugged. "I don't like to carry too much," he said. "It spoils the walk."

"But what if it rains?"

Case grinned, rubbing his hands free of crumbs. "I don't melt."

His grandfather, Peter remembered, used to make a meal of fried egg on bread. Before or after chores. And his grandfather had a rule about Sundays: walking was fine, he often strolled about the farm with Peter; but he wouldn't let you carry anything. If you carried something, a gun or fishing rod, for instance, that was work. Strange how all this came back now. He wouldn't write any checks or pay bills on Sunday either. On Sunday, he used to say, a Christian man should walk without a burden, to show he was a Christian.

"Ever done any climbing before?"

"A little," Case said.

"Where? The Alps?"

"A little. Mostly in the Himalayas."

"Oh," Peter said. He walked on in silence, feeling suddenly out of breath.

In the woods a few maples were tipped red and gold. Gray clouds hung over Mt. Jacob, half a mile above them and miles to the north, but with the exercise Peter grew warm. He took his wool shirt off and tied it around his waist, trudging along with his eyes on the gravel lane. Soon the road turned north along the edge of the mountains; a footpath led on eastward and upward.

"Look," Case said. He pointed to where five stones, two large and three small, stood in a square rod of meadow. The small read, "Asleep in Jesus," and "In Jesus' Arms." The large ones read, "RIP." Parents and children, they had died in one winter a hundred years before.

Peter stopped for a picture. "I'm glad you saw this," he said. "My grandparents were pioneers."

Case was reading the legends on the stones. His mustache twitched as if he were about to weep. "The poor," he said. "We have them always with us, no?"

"That's right," Peter said.

They walked on, single file, Case in the lead. Peter felt ashamed; he had mentioned the pioneers only by way of bragging, because he had not climbed the Himalayas. By way of contrast, Case's quote from Scripture had struck the proper note. The path plunged upward through forests of maple, birch, and pine. As the trail grew steeper, Peter grew warmer. He felt he was working, not strolling. He felt as if his grandfather's spirit were present, walking with them, but walking next to Case, not him. After a while he threw away his stick and tried to walk less on his heels and more on the balls of his feet, like Case.

In an hour they were at the top of Mt. Worth, 3000 feet, higher than Peter had ever been, except in a plane. During the climb he learned that Case was a medical student and that he had a girl friend, someone he had met in Greece. He was postponing marriage, he said, because if you marry you have to think too much about money and not enough about your calling. He was speaking only for himself, he added. Peter had once begun to study medicine, largely because he thought he would be treated better in the draft. Then came marriage, the Korean War, children, a mortgage. He said nothing, saving his breath for the climb.

On the Long Trail, going north along the tops of the ridges, walking was easier. Case's rubber soles squeaked over rocks and slipped easily over logs crisscrossing the trail. Peter kept his eyes on the bouncing canvas heels.

"Do you like medicine?" he said.

"Not really. I prefer to study language."

"Language? Why?"

"In language," Case said, as if he had given the matter some thought, "you find a people's soul."

They zig-zagged up a long cliff, then down a granite pathway between stunted pines. It was a new thought to Peter. He would have said you put your soul into action, not words. But he remembered how his grandfather used English for business, Dutch for prayer. When he could get his breath he asked,

"You're giving up medicine, then?"

"No. I will still study medicine."

"But why? If you don't like it?"

The trail went constantly up and down, winding around the shoulders of the mountains. "Like the Himalayas, you know? Always when you think you're there, another peak." Case's voice drifted back like a ghost, lingering where his body had been on the leaf-speckled sunlight of the trail. "The people in the Himalayas are very poor. For two rupees they give you fire, supper, breakfast. Lodging for you and your donkey. They are often sick."

"You mean a medical missionary?" Peter imagined himself living that life, like the life of Jesus, living among the poor, knowing their language, riding a donkey, healing them.

"I want to learn their language," Case said, "and go back."

For him, Peter thought, it was too late. Perhaps his son could do something like that. He would have to save the money.

"I think that's really great," he said, but Case had stopped and he almost ran into him. The trail had broadened into lookout, and a view of the valley, with farms and towns and church spires rising from the fields, pointing to the clouds that floated toward them, was spread below, westward to Lake Champlain.

"Our mother the earth," Case said.

Peter took another picture. Halfway through the process—reading the light meter, making his adjustments—he became aware of Case watching him, and he saw himself in the eyes of this footloose young European: middle-aged, gadget-ridden, materialistic. All the bad things people thought of when they said, *American.*

His grandmother, he remembered, used to warn him not to marry "an American," and he had obeyed her. But what would she say if she knew he had become an American himself?

By one o'clock they had climbed Mt. Jacob. They rested there, their shirts, wet with sweat, drying in the sun. In the log shelter marking the summit they found a packet of rice and a note: "This is for whoever needs it. Amen." Having nothing to cook it in, they shared Peter's candy and raisins and drank water from a spring which Case found. They rested on the hardpacked earth and talked. Case told what he had seen on his trip around the world, by tramp steamer, on foot, and by thumb: Asia, South America, the Near East. The poverty, the aspiration. What he would do. Peter hadn't much to tell: how his grandparents came from Holland and farmed, and his parents sold the farm for real estate, and one thing led to another and here he was. Working for the buck, he said apologetically. But he gave much of it to the church and the school.

" 'Give what you have, you're worthy to live,' " Case said. "That's a proverb."

Peter remembered the proverb. His grandfather used to say it in Dutch.

The summit was over 4000 feet high, and from it they could look back on the other peaks, Mt. Romance,

Mt. Worth, Burnt Hill, and on the valleys east and west. People must have called it Mt. Jacob because it seemed like a ladder to heaven. Clouds whistled above them, a few yards from their eyes. Peter could see his life spread before him, and he suddenly felt he knew what he was working for, where his life had come from, where it might lead. He was glad he had come along. He could hardly have found a better companion, he thought.

"Do you know any poetry?" Case said. "American, I mean?"

After a moment Peter said, " 'Whose woods these are I think I know.' " He had read it on a place-mat at the inn.

Case laughed and jumped to his feet. "I prefer your Walt Whitman! 'Shoulder your duds, my son, and let us be off! Look for me under your bootsoles!' "

They signed their names in a logbook in the shelter: Peter his full name, plus "Chicago, Illinois." Case wrote only his Christian name, no address. He spelled his name "Kees."

For an hour they rested and explored the summit. Peter got a shot of the elevation notice, another of the shelter where procupines had gnawed it, and several of the view. Then, with the sun beginning to sink, they started down.

On the way back they had an adventure. According to the maps they were on the Mt. Jacob Trail, which should have led back to the Burying-ground Road. Instead it began curving north, away from the inn. Great gashes crossed it periodically, bulldozed out of the woods to prevent water from flowing too swiftly downward; they had to jump into the muddy bottoms and climb out again. The air grew warmer, and a deerfly pestered them in turn, circling first one head and then the other. The wet, newly scraped path showed the tracks of deer and raccoon, and once the five-clawed print of a bear. They were in birch again, and then maple, but always going northward, on the wrong side of a fast-moving river.

"The map is no good," Peter said finally. The man at the inn had warned him that the off-trails changed every year. At last they crossed the river on foot (Peter carrying his boots, Case splashing through in his sneakers) and headed west through the woods, making their own trail through swampy underbrush and fallen trees to where they thought they had seen a new gravel road from the mountain.

It was there. It was there! They stood for a while without moving, enjoying the flat surface under their feet. They made jokes about the bear track, which neither had dared mention while they were in the woods. They hiked side by side down the long empty road, Peter peeling off his sweatshirt and tying that too around his waist.

After another hour they reached a main road, blacktop. Here he took Case's advice and walked backward, holding up his thumb, whenever a car appeared. It had been a long day, and his feet hurt, but he had never been happier. He felt ten years younger. It had been perhaps twenty years, he thought, since he had walked like this, thumbs up, trusting himself completely to strangers. Case began whistling a strange tune, a Greek tune, he said. Peter remembered, from his childhood, a song that seemed appropriate to the day. If your soul was in language, this was his soul. "Here's a poem for you," he said, and he sang aloud, in time with his moving feet,

Climbing up the mountain children
Oh Lord I didn't come here for to stay

Oh brother if I never more see you again
Gonna meet you at the Judgment Day.

"Are you Christian?" Case said suddenly.

"Yes," Peter said. He was pleased that the confession came so easily, a natural part of the day they had shared. He felt as if it were not the spirit of his grandfather only that had walked with them, or the spirit of Frost and Whitman, but Christ Himself. As if completing a liturgy, he offered Case the chance for his own confession. "And you?"

"No," Case said.

For a moment Peter could not believe what he had heard. Then he could not accept it.

"No? But why? Why not?"

"I just don't believe," Case said. "I am an atheist."

His calmness was exasperating. For Peter the day's Sabbath calm had evaporated. "But why?" he repeated. "How can you be an atheist?"

"I can't explain. There are too many—" Case shook his head. "How can you be Christian?"

Peter could not explain it; he just was. They walked on with no sound but the wind and the twittering of tiny Vermont birds, and the song kept running through Peter's head: *gonna meet you at the Judgment Day.*

Then their first ride came by, a man in coveralls in a pickup truck. He had a bow and arrows in the front seat, and on Sundays he liked to practice on muskrats while waiting for deer and bear season. Nothing illegal, he kept assuring them—as though they were two prophets come down from the mountain to judge him. He let them out on a corner some miles below the inn, and they stood on the road again, thumbs up.

Here I am bumming rides with an atheist, Peter thought. A mustached, atheist student.

They caught a last ride with two of the brokers returning from golf. The golfers, sunburned and smelling of beer, were full of admiration for their hike. That takes a lot of spirit, they said, and suddenly both of them began singing Peter's song. "Climbin' up the mountain, chillun! Oh Lawdy, didn't come here for to stay!" They figured the hike for at least fifteen miles, while they, with their golf carts, hadn't walked a tenth of that.

"And didn't get as high, either," one of them laughed.

Peter wondered whether Case had been about to say, *too many phony Christians.* That was what his grandfather said once, when he asked him why he had left Holland.

The two got off at the inn and said good-bye. Case had to pack to catch a bus to New York; Peter had to clean up for dinner. It was a pleasure, Case said, and Peter agreed. He couldn't deny that; his whole body ached pleasantly, and his appetite was enormous. They shook hands and Peter went upstairs, wondering whether he and Case would ever see each other again, and what they would say to each other if they did.

Does self-sacrifice for togetherness mean you avoid discussing your faith?

The Man He Killed

'Had he and I but met
By some old ancient inn,
We should have sat us down to wet
Right many a nipperkin!

'But ranged as infantry,
And staring face to face,
I shot at him as he at me,
And killed him in his place.

'I shot him dead because—
Because he was my foe,
Just so: my foe of course he was;
That's clear enough; although

'He thought he'd 'list, perhaps,
Off-hand like—just as I—
Was out of work—had sold his traps—
No other reason why.

'Yes; quaint and curious war is!
You shoot a fellow down
You'd treat if met where any bar is,
Or help to half-a-crown.'

Thomas Hardy

The Sniper

Liam O'Flaherty

In the early 1920's, after the Irish had won independence for most of Ireland from the English, a bloody civil war broke out between two groups of Irish patriots. Once Republicans and Free Staters had fought side by side. Now they were fighting each other. Dublin, capital of the Free State, was the scene of bitter battles.

The long June twilight faded into night. Dublin lay enveloped in darkness but for the dim light of the moon that shone through fleecy clouds, casting a pale light as of approaching dawn over the streets and the dark waters of the Liffey. Around the beleaguered Four Courts the heavy guns roared. Here and there through the city machine guns and rifles broke the silence of the night spasmodically, like dogs barking on lone farms. Republicans and Free Staters were waging civil war.

On a rooftop near O'Connell Bridge a Republican sniper lay watching. Beside him lay his rifle, and over his shoulders were slung a pair of field glasses. His face was the face of a student—thin and ascetic—but his eyes had the cold gleam of the fanatic. They were deep and thoughtful, the eyes of a man who is used to looking at death.

He was eating a sandwich hungrily. He had eaten nothing since morning. He had been too excited to eat. He finished the sandwich, and taking a flask of whiskey from his pocket, he took a short draught. Then he returned the flask to his pocket. He paused for a moment, considering whether he should risk a smoke. It was dangerous. The flash might be seen in the darkness, and there were enemies watching. He decided to take the risk. Placing a cigarette between his lips, he struck a match, inhaled the smoke hurriedly, and put out the light. Almost immediately, a bullet flattened itself against the parapet of the roof. The sniper took another whiff and put out the cigarette. Then he swore softly and crawled away to the left.

Cautiously he raised himself and peered over the parapet. There was a flash, and a bullet whizzed over his head. He dropped immediately. He had seen the flash. It came from the opposite side of the street.

He rolled over the roof to a chimney stack in the rear and slowly drew himself up behind it until his eyes were level with the top of the parapet. There was nothing to be seen—just the dim outline of the opposite housetop against the blue sky. His enemy was under cover.

Just then an armored car came across the bridge and advanced slowly up the street. It stopped on the opposite side of the street fifty yards ahead. The sniper could hear the dull panting of the motor. His heart beat faster. It was an enemy car. He wanted to fire, but he knew it was useless. His bullets would never pierce the steel that covered the gray monster.

Then round the corner of a side street came an old woman, her head covered by a tattered shawl. She began to talk to the man in the turret of the car. She was pointing to the roof where the sniper lay. An informer.

The turret opened. A man's head and shoulders appeared looking towards the sniper. The sniper raised his rifle and fired. The head fell heavily on the turret wall. The woman darted toward the side street. The sniper fired again. The woman whirled round and fell with a shriek into the gutter.

Suddenly from the opposite roof a shot rang out, and the sniper dropped his rifle with a curse. The rifle clattered to the roof. The sniper thought the noise would wake the dead. He stopped to pick the rifle up.

He couldn't lift it. His forearm was dead. He muttered, "I'm hit."

Dropping flat onto the roof, he crawled back to the parapet. With his left hand he felt the injured right forearm. The blood was oozing through the sleeve of his coat. There was no pain—just a deadened sensation, as if the arm had been cut off.

Quickly he drew his knife from his pocket, opened it on the breastwork of the parapet, and ripped open the sleeve. There was a small hole where the bullet had entered. On the other side there was no hole. The bullet had lodged in the bone. It must have fractured it. He bent the arm below the wound. The arm bent back easily. He ground his teeth to overcome the pain.

Then, taking out his field dressing, he ripped open the packet with his knife. He broke the neck of the iodine bottle and let the bitter fluid drip into the wound. A paroxysm of pain swept through him. He placed the cotton wadding over the wound and wrapped the dressing over it. He tied the end with his teeth. Then he lay still against the parapet, and closing his eyes, he made an effort of will to overcome the pain.

In the street beneath all was still. The armored car had retired speedily over the bridge, with the machine gunner's head hanging lifeless over the turret. The woman's corpse lay still in the gutter.

The sniper lay for a long time nursing his wounded arm and planning escape. Morning must not find him wounded on the roof. The enemy on the opposite roof covered his escape. He must kill that enemy, and he could not use his rifle. He had only a revolver to do it. Then he thought of a plan.

Taking off his cap, he placed it over the muzzle of his

rifle. Then he pushed the rifle slowly upwards over the parapet until the cap was visible from the opposite side of the street. Almost immediately there was a report, and a bullet pierced the center of the cap. The sniper slanted the rifle forward. The cap slipped down into the street. Then, catching the rifle in the middle, the sniper dropped his left hand over the roof and let it hang, lifelessly. After a few moments he let the rifle drop to the street. Then he sank to the roof, dragging his hand with him.

Crawling quickly to the left, he peered up at the corner of the roof. His ruse had succeeded. The other sniper, seeing the cap and rifle fall, thought that he had killed his man. He was now standing before a row of chimney pots, looking across, with his head clearly silhouetted against the western sky.

The Republican sniper smiled and lifted his revolver above the edge of the parapet. The distance was about fifty yards—a hard shot in the dim light—and his right arm was paining him like a thousand devils. He took a steady aim. His hand trembled with eagerness. Pressing his lips together, he took a deep breath through his nostrils and fired. He was almost deafened with the report, and his arm shook with the recoil.

Then, when the smoke cleared, he peered across and uttered a cry of joy. His enemy had been hit. He was reeling over the parapet in his death agony. He struggled to keep his feet, but he was slowly falling forward, as if in a dream. The rifle fell from his grasp, hit the parapet, fell over, bounded off the pole of a barber's shop beneath, and then cluttered onto the pavement.

Then the dying man on the roof crumpled up and fell forward. The body turned over and over in space and hit the ground with a dull thud. Then it lay still.

The sniper looked at his enemy falling, and he shuddered. The lust of battle died in him. He became bitten by remorse. The sweat stood out in beads on his forehead. Weakened by his wound and the long summer day of fasting and watching on the roof, he revolted from the sight of the shattered mass of his dead enemy. His teeth chattered. He began to gibber to himself, cursing the war, cursing himself, cursing everybody.

He looked at the smoking revolver in his hand, and with an oath he hurled it to the roof at his feet. The revolver went off with the concussion, and the bullet whizzed past the sniper's head. He was frightened back to his senses by the shock. His nerves steadied. The cloud of fear scattered from his mind, and he laughed.

Taking the whiskey flask from his pocket, he emptied it at a draught. He felt reckless under the influence of the spirits. He decided to leave the roof and look for his company commander to report. Everywhere around was quiet. There was not much danger in going through the streets. He picked up his revolver and put it in his pocket. Then he crawled down through the skylight to the house underneath.

When the sniper reached the laneway on the street level, he felt a sudden curiosity as to the identity of the enemy sniper whom he had killed. He decided that he was a good shot whoever he was. He wondered if he knew him. Perhaps he had been in his own company before the split in the army. He decided to risk going over to have a look at him. He peered around the corner into O'Connell Street. In the upper part of the street there was heavy firing, but around here all was quiet.

The sniper darted across the street. A machine gun tore up the ground around him with a hail of bullets, but he escaped. He threw himself downwards beside the corpse. The machine gun stopped.

Then the sniper turned over the dead body and looked into his brother's face.

Why did the author wait until the very end to mention "brother"? What's your reaction to discovering that fact?

Hate

My enemy came nigh,
And I
Stared fiercely in his face.
My lips went writhing back in a grimace,
And stern I watched him with a narrow eye.
Then, as I turned away, my enemy,
That bitter heart and savage, said to me:
"Some day, when this is past,
When all the arrows that we have are cast,
We may ask one another why we hate,
And fail to find a story to relate.
It may seem to us then a mystery
That we could hate each other."

Thus said he,
And did not turn away,
Waiting to hear what I might have to say.
But I fled quickly, fearing if I stayed
I might have kissed him as I would a maid.

James Stephens

THE LAST FLOWER

A PARABLE IN PICTURES

By

James Thurber

WORLD WAR XII, AS EVERYBODY KNOWS,

BROUGHT ABOUT THE COLLAPSE OF CIVILIZATION

TOWNS, CITIES, AND VILLAGES DISAPPEARED FROM THE EARTH

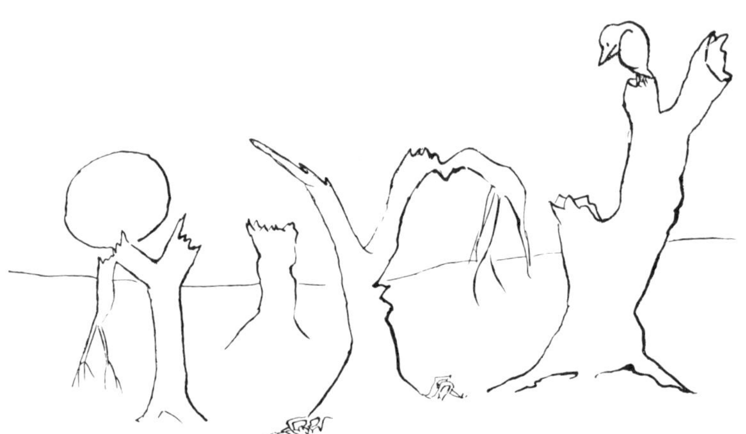

ALL THE GROVES AND FORESTS WERE DESTROYED

AND ALL THE GARDENS

AND ALL THE WORKS OF ART

MEN, WOMEN, AND CHILDREN BECAME LOWER THAN THE LOWER ANIMALS

DISCOURAGED AND DISILLUSIONED, DOGS DESERTED THEIR FALLEN MASTERS

EMBOLDENED BY THE PITIFUL CONDITION OF THE FORMER LORDS OF THE EARTH, RABBITS DESCENDED UPON THEM

BOOKS, PAINTINGS, AND MUSIC DISAPPEARED FROM THE EARTH, AND HUMAN BEINGS JUST SAT AROUND, DOING NOTHING

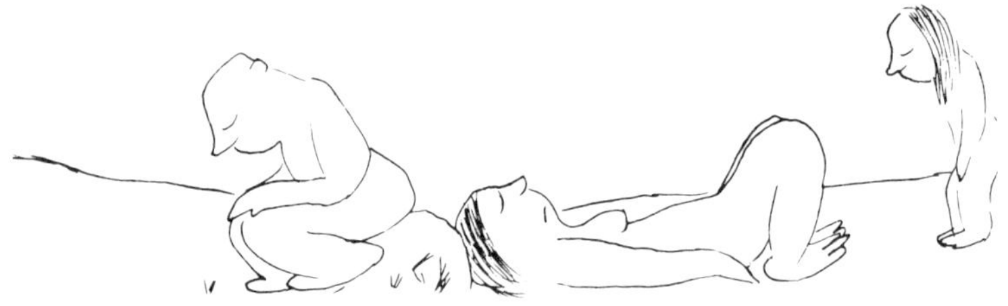

YEARS AND YEARS WENT BY

EVEN THE FEW GENERALS WHO WERE LEFT
FORGOT WHAT THE LAST WAR HAD DECIDED

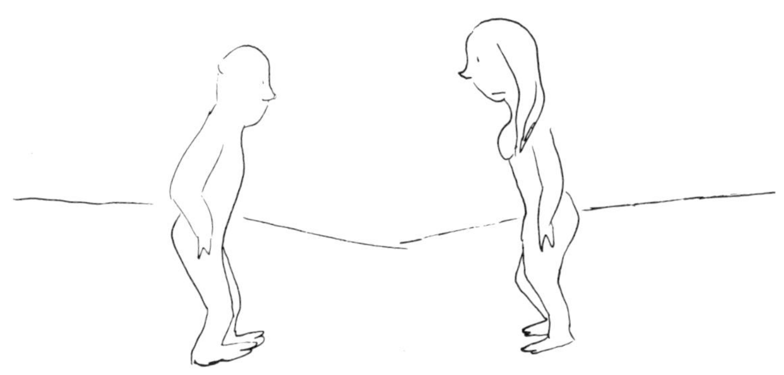

BOYS AND GIRLS GREW UP TO STARE AT EACH OTHER BLANKLY, FOR LOVE HAD PASSED FROM THE EARTH

ONE DAY A YOUNG GIRL WHO HAD NEVER SEEN A FLOWER CHANCED TO COME UPON THE LAST ONE IN THE WORLD

SHE TOLD THE OTHER HUMAN BEINGS THAT THE LAST FLOWER WAS DYING

THE ONLY ONE WHO PAID ANY ATTENTION TO HER WAS A YOUNG MAN SHE FOUND WANDERING ABOUT

TOGETHER THE YOUNG MAN AND THE GIRL NURTURED THE FLOWER AND IT BEGAN TO LIVE AGAIN

ONE DAY A BEE VISITED THE FLOWER, AND A HUMMINGBIRD

BEFORE LONG THERE WERE TWO FLOWERS, AND THEN FOUR, AND THEN A GREAT MANY

GROVES AND FORESTS FLOURISHED AGAIN

THE YOUNG GIRL BEGAN TO TAKE
AN INTEREST IN HOW SHE LOOKED

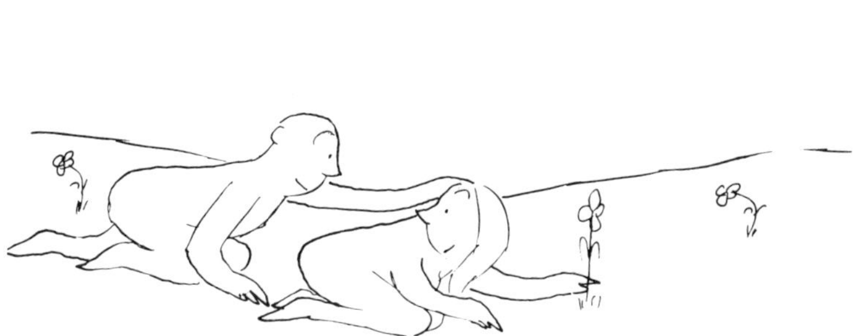

THE YOUNG MAN DISCOVERED THAT
TOUCHING THE GIRL WAS PLEASURABLE

LOVE WAS REBORN INTO THE WORLD

THEIR CHILDREN GREW UP STRONG AND HEALTHY AND LEARNED TO RUN AND LAUGH

DOGS CAME OUT OF THEIR EXILE

THE YOUNG MAN DISCOVERED, BY PUTTING ONE STONE UPON ANOTHER, HOW TO BUILD A SHELTER

PRETTY SOON EVERYBODY WAS BUILDING SHELTERS

TOWNS, CITIES, AND VILLAGES SPRANG UP

SONG CAME BACK INTO THE WORLD

AND TROUBADOURS AND JUGGLERS

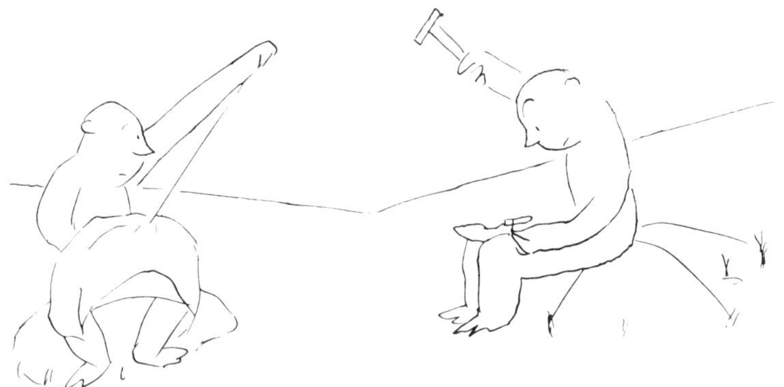

AND TAILORS AND COBBLERS

AND PAINTERS AND POETS

AND SCULPTORS AND WHEELWRIGHTS

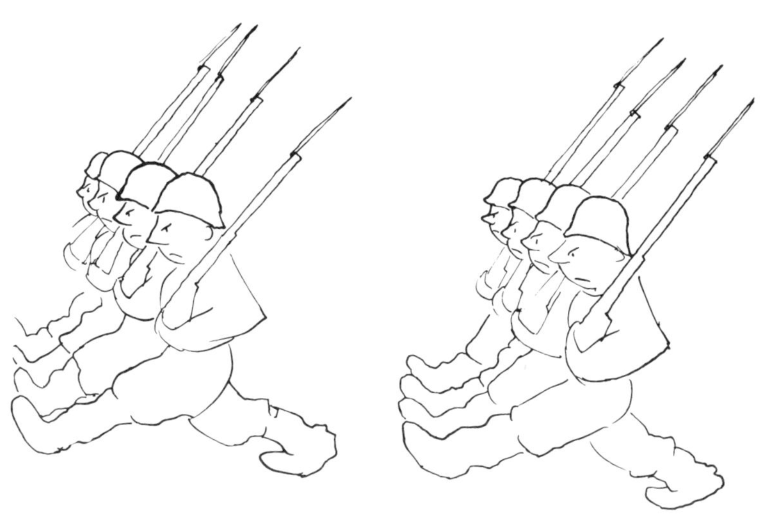

AND SOLDIERS

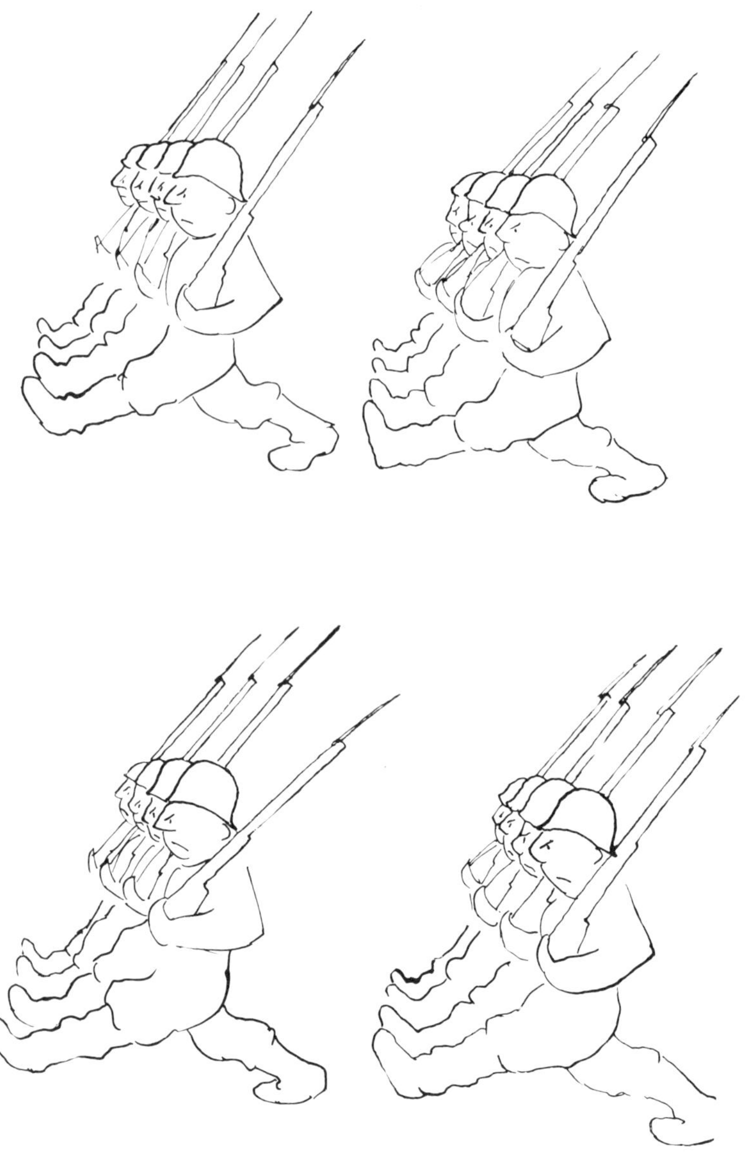

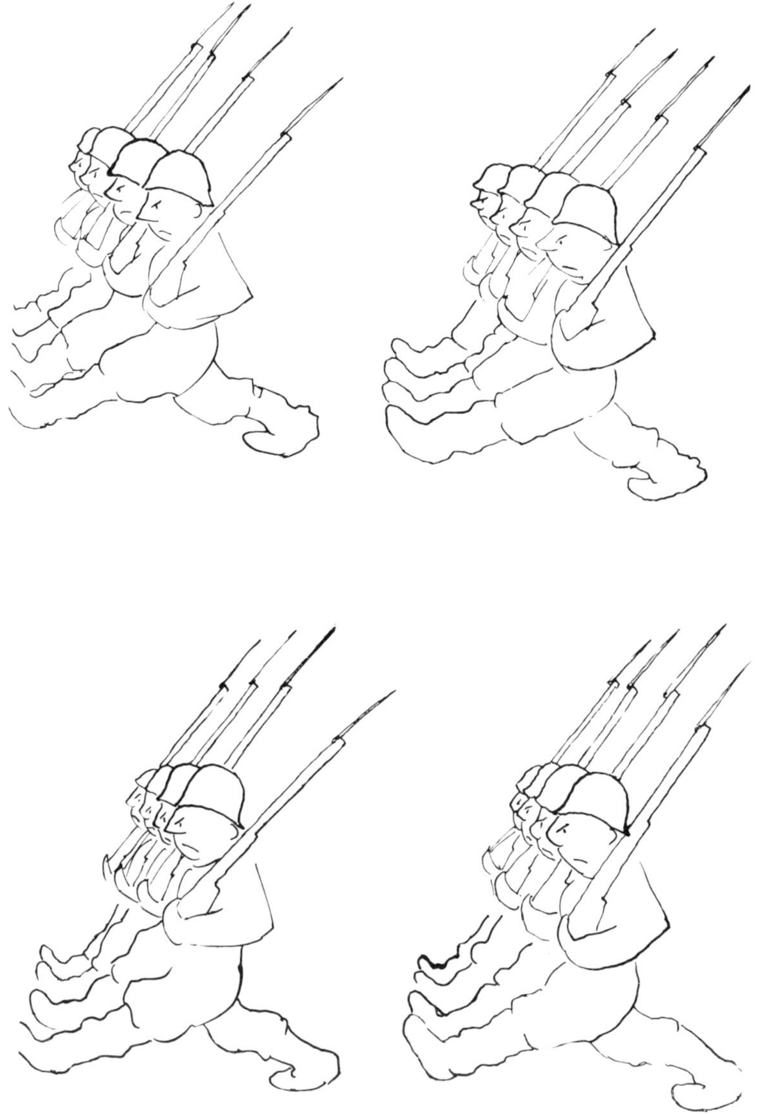

AND LIEUTENANTS AND CAPTAINS

AND GENERALS AND MAJOR-GENERALS

AND LIBERATORS

SOME PEOPLE WENT ONE PLACE TO LIVE,
AND SOME ANOTHER

BEFORE LONG, THOSE WHO WENT TO LIVE IN THE VALLEYS WISHED THEY HAD GONE TO LIVE IN THE HILLS

AND THOSE WHO HAD GONE TO LIVE IN THE HILLS WISHED THEY HAD GONE TO LIVE IN THE VALLEYS

THE LIBERATORS, UNDER THE GUIDANCE OF GOD,
SET FIRE TO THE DISCONTENT

SO PRESENTLY THE WORLD WAS AT WAR AGAIN

THIS TIME THE DESTRUCTION WAS SO COMPLETE...

THAT NOTHING AT ALL WAS LEFT IN THE WORLD

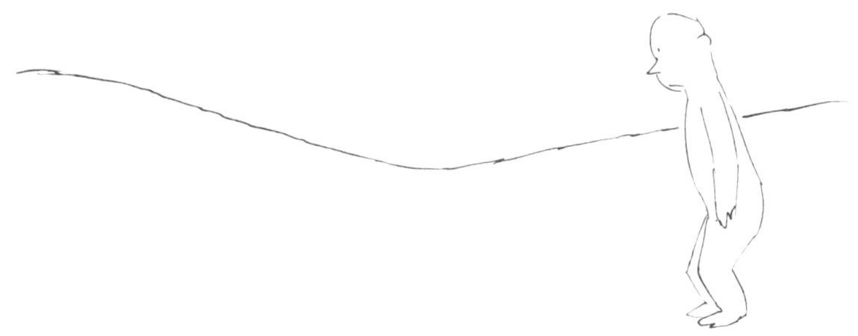

EXCEPT ONE MAN

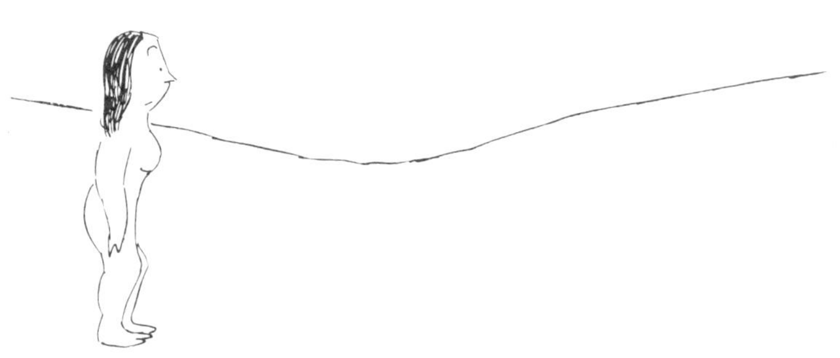

AND ONE WOMAN

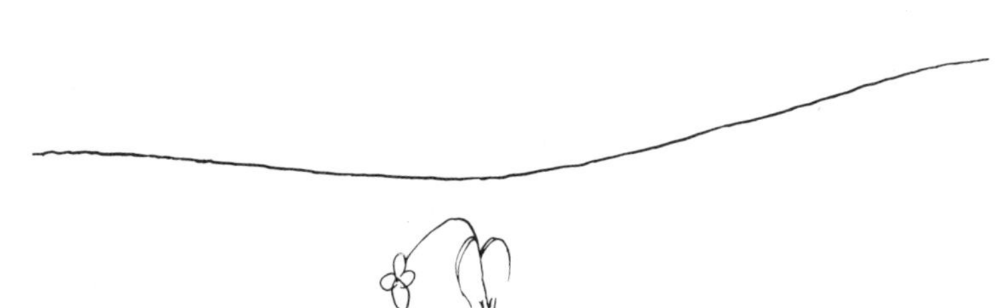

AND ONE FLOWER

Together

Choose

The single clenched fist lifted and ready,
Or the open asking hand held out and waiting.
Choose:
For we meet by one or the other.

Carl Sandburg

They Watched Her Die

A. M. Rosenthal

For more than half an hour thirty-eight respectable, law-abiding citizens in Queens watched a killer stalk and stab a woman in three separate attacks.

Twice the sound of their voices and the sudden glow of their bedroom lights interrupted him and frightened him off. Each time he returned, sought her out and stabbed her again. Not one person telephoned the police during the assault. One witness called after the woman was dead.

That was two weeks ago today. But Assistant Chief Inspector Frederick M. Lussen, in charge of Queens' detectives and a veteran of twenty-five years of homicide investigations, is still shocked.

He can usually speak quite matter-of-factly about murders. But the Queens slaying baffles him—not because it is a murder, but because the "good people" failed to call the police.

"As we have reconstructed the crime," he said, "the assailant had three chances to kill this woman during a thirty-five-minute period. He returned twice to complete the job. If we had been called when he first attacked, the woman might not be dead now."

This is what the police say happened beginning at 3:20 a.m. in the quiet, middle-class, tree-lined Austin Street area:

Twenty-eight-year-old Catherine Genovese, who was called Kitty by almost everyone in the neighborhood, was returning home from her job as manager of a bar. She parked her red Fiat in a lot next to the Kew Gardens Long Island Rail Road Station. Like many people who lived in the neighborhood, she had parked there day after day, although the railroad frowns on it.

She turned off the lights of her car, locked the door, and started to walk the 100 feet to the entrance of her apartment at 82-70 Austin Street.

The entrance to the apartment is in the rear of the building because the front is rented to stores. At night the quiet neighborhood is covered with darkness, as most residential neighborhoods are.

Miss Genovese noticed a man at the far end of the lot, near a seven-story apartment house at 82-40 Austin Street. She stopped. Then, nervously, she headed up Austin Street toward Lefferts Boulevard, where there is a call box to the 102nd Police Precinct in nearby Richmond Hill.

She got as far as a street light in front of a bookstore before the man grabbed her. She screamed. Lights went on in the ten-story apartment house at 82-67 Austin Street, which faces the bookstore. Windows slid open and voices were heard in the early morning stillness.

Miss Genovese screamed: "Oh, my God, he stabbed me! Please help me!"

From one of the upper windows in the apartment house, a man called down: "Let that girl alone!"

The assailant looked up at him, shrugged, and walked

down Austin Street toward a white car parked a short distance away. Miss Genovese struggled to her feet.

Lights went out. The killer returned to Miss Genovese, now trying to make her way around the side of the building by the parking lot to get to her apartment. The assailant stabbed her again.

"I'm dying!" she shrieked. "I'm dying!"

Windows were opened again, and lights went on in many apartments. The assailant got into his car and drove away. Miss Genovese staggered to her feet. A city bus passed. It was 3:35 a.m.

The assailant returned. By then, Miss Genovese had crawled to the back of the building, where the freshly painted doors to the apartment house held out hope of safety. The killer tried the first door. She wasn't there. At the second door, he saw her slumped on the floor at the foot of the stairs. He stabbed her a third time–fatally.

It was 3:50 by the time the police received their first call from a man who was a neighbor of Miss Genovese. In two minutes they were at the scene. The neighbor, a seventy-year-old woman, and another woman were the only persons on the street. Nobody else came forward.

The man explained that he had called the police after much thought. He had phoned a friend for advice and then he had crossed the roof of the building to the apartment of the elderly woman to get her to make the call.

"I didn't want to get involved," he told the police.

Six days later the police arrested a man who confessed to killing two other women in addition to Miss Genovese.

The police told how simple it would have been to have gotten in touch with them. "A phone call," said one of the detectives, "would have done it."

Can the witnesses be held legally responsible in any way for not reporting the crime?

The Police Department's legal bureau said, "There is no legal responsibility for any citizen to report a crime."

Today witnesses from the neighborhood, which is made up of expensive houses, find it hard to explain why they didn't call the police.

Lieutenant Bernard Jacobs, who handled the case, said:

"It's one of the better neighborhoods. There are few reports of crimes. You only get the usual complaints about boys playing or garbage cans being turned over."

The police said most people had told them they had been afraid to call, but could not tell what they had been afraid of.

"We can understand why people don't want to be involved where the violence is taking place," Lieutenant Jacobs said, "but where they are in their homes, near phones, why should they be afraid to call the police?"

He said his men were able to piece together what happened—and capture the suspect—because the residents furnished all the information when detectives rang doorbells during the days following the slaying.

"But why didn't someone call us that night?" he asked unbelievingly.

Witnesses—some of them unable to believe what they had allowed to happen—told a reporter why.

A housewife casually said, "We thought it was a lover's quarrel." A husband and wife both said, "Frankly, we were afraid." They seemed aware of the fact that they might have saved the girl. A woman who was very upset said, "I didn't want my husband to get involved."

One couple, now willing to talk about that night, said they heard the first screams. The husband looked at the bookstore where the killer first grabbed Miss Genovese.

"We went to the window to see what was happening," he said, "but the light from our bedroom made it difficult to see the street." The wife, still nervous, added: "I put out the light and we were able to see better." Asked why they hadn't called the police, she shrugged and replied, "I don't know."

A man peeked out from an opening in his door and told the story of the killer's second attack. Why hadn't he called the police at the time? "I was tired," he said, without emotion. "I went back to bed."

It was 4:25 a.m. when the ambulance arrived for the body of Miss Genovese. It drove off. "Then," a solemn police detective said, "the people came out."

A Helping Hand

We gave a helping hand to grass—
    and it turned into corn.
We gave a helping hand to fire—
    and it turned into a rocket.
Hesitatingly,
cautiously,
we give a helping hand
to people,
to some people . . .

Miroslav Holub

Why do you think we exclude some people from the helping hand?

Loneliness

I was about to go, and said so;
And I had almost started for the door.
But he was all alone in the sugar-house,
And more lonely than he'd ever been before.
We'd talked for half an hour, almost,
About the price of sugar, and how I like my school,
And he had made me drink some syrup hot,
Telling me it was better that way than when cool.

And I agreed, and thanked him for it,
And said good-bye, and was about to go.
Want to see where I was born?
He asked me quickly. How to say no?

The sugar-house looked over miles of valley.
He pointed with a sticky finger to a patch of snow
Where he was born. The house, he said, was gone.
I can understand these people better, now I know.

Brooks Jenkins

To communicate is the beginning of understanding.

A Time to Talk

When a friend calls to me from the road
And slows his horse to a meaning walk,
I don't stand still and look around
On all the hills I haven't hoed,
And shout from where I am, "What is it?"
No, not as there is a time to talk.
I thrust my hoe in the mellow ground,
Blade-end up and five feet tall,
And plod: I go up to the stone wall
For a friendly visit.

Robert Frost

Split Cherry Tree

Jesse Stuart

"I don't mind staying after school," I says to Professor Herbert, "but I'd rather you'd whip me with a switch and let me go home early. Pa will whip me anyway for getting home two hours late."

"You are too big to whip," says Professor Herbert, "and I have to punish you for climbing up in that cherry tree. You boys knew better than that! The other five boys have paid their dollar each. You have been the only one who has not helped pay for the tree. Can't you borrow a dollar?"

"I can't," I says. "I'll have to take the punishment. I wish it would be quicker punishment. I wouldn't mind."

Professor Herbert stood and looked at me. He was a big man. He wore a grey suit of clothes. The suit matched his grey hair.

"You don't know my father," I says to Professor Herbert. "He might be called a little old-fashioned. He makes us mind him until we're twenty-one years old. He believes: 'If you spare the rod you spoil the child.' I'll never be able to make him understand about the cherry tree. I'm the first of my people to go to high school."

"You must take the punishment," says Professor Herbert. "You must stay two hours after school today and two hours after school tomorrow. I am allowing you twenty-five cents an hour. That is good money for a high school student. You can sweep the schoolhouse floor, wash the blackboards, and clean windows. I'll pay the dollar for you."

I couldn't ask Professor Herbert to loan me a dollar. He never offered to loan it to me. I had to stay and help the janitor and work out my fine at a quarter an hour.

It was six o'clock when I left the schoolhouse. I had six miles to walk home. It would be after seven when I got home. I had all my work to do when I got home. It took Pa and me both to do the work. Seven cows to milk. Nineteen head of cattle to feed, four mules, twenty-five hogs, firewood and stovewood to cut, and water to draw from the well. He would be doing it when I got home. He would be mad and wondering what was keeping me!

I hurried home. I had to run. I ran across the pasture to the house. I threw down my books in the chipyard. I ran out to the barn. I saw Pa spreading fodder on the ground to the cattle. That was my job. I ran up to the fence. I says: "Leave that for me, Pa. I'll do it. I'm just a little late."

"I see you are," says Pa. He turned and looked at me. His eyes danced fire. "What in th' world has kept you so? Why ain't you been here to help me with this work? Make a gentleman out'n one boy in th' family and this is what you get! Send you to high school and you get too onery fer th' buzzards to smell!"

I never said anything. I didn't want to tell why I was late from school. Pa stopped scattering the bundles of fodder. He looked at me. He says: "Why are you gettin' in here this time o' night? You tell me or I'll take a hickory withe to you right here on th' spot!"

I says: "I had to stay after school." I couldn't lie to Pa. He'd go to school and find out why I had to stay. If I lied to him it would be too bad for me.

"Why did you haf to stay after school?" says Pa.

I says: "Our biology class went on a field trip today. Six of us boys broke down a cherry tree. We had to give a dollar apiece to pay for the tree. I didn't have the dollar. Professor Herbert is making me work out my dollar. He gives me twenty-five cents an hour. I had to stay in this afternoon. I'll have to stay in tomorrow afternoon!"

"Are you telling me th' truth?" says Pa.

"I'm telling you the truth," I says. "Go and see for yourself."

"That's just what I'll do in th' mornin'," says Pa. "Jist whose cherry tree did you break down?"

"Eif Crabtree's cherry tree!"

"What was you doin' clear out in Eif Crabtree's place?" says Pa. "He lives four miles from th' County High School. Don't they teach you no books at that high school? Do they jist let you get out and gad over th' hillsides? If that's all they do I'll keep you at home, Dave. I've got work here for you to do!"

"Pa," I says, "Spring is just getting here. We take a subject in school where we have to have bugs, snakes, flowers, lizards, frogs, and plants. It is biology. It was a pretty day today. We went out to find a few of these. Six of us boys saw a lizard at the same time sunning on a cherry tree. We all went up the tree to get it. We broke the tree down. It split at the forks. Eif Crabtree was plowing down below us. He ran up the hill and got our names. The other boys gave their dollar apiece. I didn't have mine. Professor Herbert put mine in for me. I have to work it out at school."

"Poor man's son, huh," says Pa. "I'll attend to that myself in th' mornin'. I'll take keer o' 'im. He ain't from this county nohow. I'll go down there in th' mornin' and see 'im. Lettin' you leave your books and galavant all over th' hills. What kind of a school is it nohow! Didn't do that, my son, when I's a little shaver in school. All fared alike too."

"Pa, please don't go down there," I says. "Just let me have fifty cents and pay the rest of my fine! I don't want you to go down there! I don't want you to start anything with Professor Herbert!"

I thought once I'd run through the woods above the barn just as hard as I could go. I thought I'd leave high school and home forever! Pa could not catch me! I'd get away! I couldn't go back to school with him. He'd have a gun and maybe he'd shoot Professor Herbert. It was hard to tell what he would do. I could tell Pa that school had changed in the hills from the way it was when he was a boy but he wouldn't understand. I could tell him we studied frogs, birds, snakes, lizards, flowers, insects. But Pa wouldn't understand. If I did run away from home it wouldn't matter to Pa. He would see Professor Herbert anyway. He would think that high school and Professor Herbert had run me away from home. There was no need to run away. I'd just have to stay, finish foddering the cattle, and go to school with Pa the next morning.

The moon shone bright in the cold March sky. I finished my work by moonlight. Professor Herbert really didn't know how much work I had to do at home. If he had known he would not have kept me after school. He would have loaned me a dollar to have paid my part on the cherry tree. He had never lived in the hills. He didn't know the way the hill boys had to work so that they could go to school. Now he was teaching in a County High School where all the boys who attended were from hill farms.

After I'd finished doing my work I went to the house and ate my supper. Pa and Mom had eaten. My supper was getting cold. I heard Pa and Mom talking in the front room. Pa was telling Mom about me staying in after school.

"I had to do all th' milkin' tonight, chop th' wood myself. It's too hard on me after I've turned ground all day. I'm goin' to take a day off tomorrow and see if I can't remedy things a little. I'll go down to that high school tomorrow. I won't be a very good scholar fer Professor Herbert nohow. He won't keep me in atter school. I'll take a different kind of lesson down there and make 'im acquainted with it."

"Now Luster," says Mom, "you jist stay away from there. Don't cause a lot o' trouble. You can be jailed fer a trick like that. You'll get th' Law atter you. You'll jist go down there and show off and plague your own boy Dave to death in front o' all th' scholars!"

"Plague or no plague," says Pa, "he don't take into consideration what all I haf to do here, does he? I'll show 'im it ain't right to keep one boy in and let the rest go scot free. My boy is good as th' rest, ain't he? A bullet will make a hole in a schoolteacher same as it will anybody else. He can't do me that way and get by with it. I'll plug 'im first. I aim to go down there bright and early in the mornin' and get all this straight! I aim to see about bug larnin' and this runnin' all over creation huntin' snakes, lizards, and frogs. Ransackin' th' country and goin' through cherry orchards and breakin' th' trees down atter lizards! Old Eif Crabtree ought to a-poured th' hot lead to 'em instead o' chargin' six dollars fer th' tree! He ought to a-got old Herbert th' first one!"

Pa got up at four o'clock. He built a fire in the stove. Then he built a fire in the fireplace. He got Mom up to get breakfast. Then he got me up to help feed and milk. By the time we had our work done at the barn, Mom had breakfast for us. We ate our breakfast. Daylight came and we could see the bare oak trees covered with frost.

"Now Dave," says Pa, "let's get ready fer school. I aim to go with you this mornin' and look into bug larnin', frog larnin', lizard and snake larnin', and breakin' down cherry trees! I don't like no sicha foolish way o' larnin' myself!" We started trudging toward the high school across the hill.

It was early when we got to the school. Professor Herbert had just got there. I thought as we walked up the steps into the schoolhouse: "Maybe Pa will find out Professor Herbert is a good man. He just doesn't know him. Just like I felt toward the Lambert boys across the hill. I didn't like them until I'd seed them and talked to them. After I went to school with them and talked to them, I liked them and we were friends. It's a lot in knowing the other fellow."

"You're th' Professor here, ain't you?" says Pa.

"Yes," says Professor Herbert, "and you are Dave's father."

"Yes," says Pa, pulling out his gun and laying it on the seat in Professor Herbert's office. Professor Herbert's eyes got big behind his black-rimmed glasses when he saw Pa's gun. Color came into his pale cheeks.

"Jist a few things about this school I want to know," says Pa. "I'm tryin' to make a scholar out'n Dave. He's the only one out'n eleven youngins I've sent to high school. Here he comes in late and leaves me all th' work to do! He said you's all out bug huntin' yesterday and broke a cherry tree down. He had to stay two hours after school yesterday and work out money to pay on that cherry tree! Is that right?"

"Wwwwy," says Professor Herbert, "I guess it is."

"Well," says Pa, "this ain't no high school. It's a bug school, a lizard school, a snake school! It ain't no school nohow!"

"Why did you bring that gun?" says Professor Herbert to Pa.

"You see that little hole," says Pa as he picked up the

long blue forty-four and put his finger on the end of the barrel, "a bullet can come out'n that hole that will kill a schoolteacher same as it will any other man. It will kill a rich man same as a poor man. But atter I come in and saw you, I know'd I wouldn't need it. This maul o' mine could do you up in a few minutes."

Pa stood there, big, hard, brown-skinned, and mighty beside of Professor Herbert. I didn't know Pa was so much bigger and harder. I'd never seen Pa in a schoolhouse before. I'd seen Professor Herbert. He always looked big before to me. He didn't look big standing beside of Pa.

"I was only doing my duty, Mr. Sexton," says Professor Herbert, "and following the course of study the state provided us with."

"Course o' study," says Pa. "What study, bug study? Varmint study?"

Students were coming into the schoolhouse now. Professor Herbert says: "Close the door, Dave, so others won't hear."

I walked over and closed the door. I was shaking like a leaf in the wind. I thought Pa was going to hit Professor Herbert every minute. He was doing all the talking. His face was getting red. The red color was coming through the brown weather-beaten skin on Pa's face.

"What else could I have done with Dave, Mr. Sexton?" says Professor Herbert. "The boys didn't have any business all climbing that cherry tree after one lizard. One boy could have gone up in the tree and got it. The farmer charged us six dollars. It was a little steep, I think, but we had it to pay. Must I make five boys pay and let your boy off? He said he didn't have the dollar and couldn't get it. So I put it in for him. I'm letting him work it out. He's not working for me. He's working for the school!"

"It jist didn't look fair to me! Work one and let th' rest out because they got th' money. I don't see what bugs has got to do with a high school! It don't look good to me nohow!"

Pa picked up his gun and put it back in its holster. The red color left Professor Herbert's face. He talked more to Pa. Pa softened a little. It looked funny to see Pa in the high school building. It was the first time he'd ever been there.

"We were not only hunting snakes, toads, flowers, butterflies, lizards," says Professor Herbert, "but, Mr. Sexton, I was hunting dry timothy grass to put in an incubator and raise some protozoa."

"I don't know what that is," says Pa. "Th' incubator is th' new-fangled way o' cheatin' th' hens and raisin' chickens. I ain't so sure about th' breed o' chickens you mentioned."

"You've heard of germs, Mr. Sexton, haven't you?" says Professor Herbert.

"Jist call me Luster if you don't mind," says Pa, very casual like.

"All right, Luster, you've heard of germs, haven't you?"

"Yes," says Pa, "but I don't believe in germs. I'm sixty-five years old and I ain't seen one yet!"

"You can't see them with your naked eye," says Professor Herbert. "Just keep that gun in the holster and stay with me in the high school today. I have a few things I want to show you. That scum on your teeth has germs in it."

"What," says Pa, "you mean to tell me I've got germs on my teeth!"

"Yes," says Professor Herbert. "The same kind as we

might be able to find in a living black snake if we dissect it!"

"I don't mean to dispute your word," says Pa, "but I jist don't believe it. I don't believe I have germs on my teeth!"

"Stay with me today and I'll show you. I want to take you through the school anyway! School has changed a lot in the hills since you went to school. I don't guess we had high schools in this county when you went to school!"

'No," says Pa, "jist readin', writin', and cipherin'. We didn't have all this bug larnin', frog larnin', and findin' germs on your teeth and in the middle o' black snakes! Th' world's changin'."

"It is," says Professor Herbert, "and we hope all for the better. Boys like your own there are going to help change it. He knows all what I've told you. You stay with me today."

"I'll shore stay with you," says Pa. "I jist want to see a germ. I've never seen one in my life. 'Seein' is believin',' Pap allus told me."

Pa walks out of the office with Professor Herbert. I just hoped Professor Herbert didn't have Pa arrested for pulling his gun. Pa's gun has always been a friend to him when he goes to settle disputes.

The bell rang. School took up. I saw the students when they marched in the schoolhouse look at Pa. They would grin and punch each other. Pa just stood and watched them pass in at the schoolhouse door. Two long lines marched in the house. The boys and girls were clean and well-dressed. Pa stood over in the schoolyard under a leafless elm, in his sheepskin coat, his big boots laced in front with buckskin, and his heavy socks stuck above his boot tops. Pa's overalls legs were baggy and wrinkled between his coat and boot tops. His blue work shirt showed at the collar. His big black hat showed his grey-streaked black hair. His face was hard and weather-tanned to the color of a ripe fodder blade. His hands were big and gnarled like the roots of the elm tree he stood beside.

When I went to my first class I saw Pa and Professor Herbert going around over the schoolhouse. At noon in the high school cafeteria Pa and Professor Herbert sat together at the little table where Professor Herbert always ate by himself. They ate together. The students watched the way Pa ate. He ate with his knife instead of his fork. A lot of the students felt sorry for me after they found out he was my father. They didn't have to feel sorry for me. I wasn't ashamed of Pa after I found out he wasn't going to shoot Professor Herbert. I was glad they had made friends. I wasn't ashamed of Pa. I wouldn't be as long as he behaved.

In the afternoon when we went to biology Pa was in the class. He was sitting on one of the high stools beside the microscope. We went ahead with our work just as if Pa wasn't in the class. I saw Pa take his knife and scrape tartar from one of his teeth. Professor Herbert put it on the lens and adjusted the microscope for Pa. He adjusted it and worked awhile. Then he says: "Now, Luster, look! Put your eye right down to the light. Squint the other eye!"

Pa put his head down and did as Professor Herbert said: "I see 'im," says Pa. "Who'd a ever thought that? Right on a body's teeth! Right in a body's mouth. You're right certain they ain't no fake to this, Professor Herbert?"

"No, Luster," says Professor Herbert, "it's there. That's the germ. Germs live in a world we cannot see with the naked eye. We must use the microscope. There are millions of them in our bodies. Some are harmful. Others are helpful."

Pa holds his face down and looks through the microscope. We stop and watch Pa. He sits upon the tall stool. His knees are against the table. His legs are long. His coat slips up behind when he bends over. The handle of his gun shows. Professor Herbert pulls his coat down quickly.

"Oh, yes," says Pa. He gets up and pulls his coat down. Pa's face gets a little red. He knows about his gun and he knows he doesn't have any use for it in high school.

"We have a big black snake over here we caught yesterday," says Professor Herbert. "We'll chloroform him and dissect him and show you he has germs in his body too."

"Don't do it," says Pa. "I believe you. I jist don't want to see you kill the black snake. I like black snakes. I jist hate to see people kill 'em. I don't allow 'em killed on my place."

The students looked at Pa. They seemed to like him better after he said that. Pa with a gun in his pocket but a tender heart beneath his ribs for snakes, but not for man! Pa won't whip a mule at home. He won't whip his cattle.

Professor Herbert took Pa through the laboratory. He showed him the different kinds of work we were doing. Then they walked out together.

When our biology class was over I walked out of the room. It was our last class for the day. I got my broom and started to sweep. Professor Herbert walked up and says: "I'm going to let you do that some other time. You can go home with your father."

I laid my broom down, got my books, and went down the steps.

Pa says: "Ain't you got two hours o' sweeping yet to do?"

I says: "Professor Herbert said I could do it some other time. He said for me to go home with you."

"No," says Pa. "You are goin' to do as he says. He's a good man. School has changed from my day and time. I'm a dead leaf, Dave: I'm behind. I don't belong here. If he'll let me I'll get a broom and we'll both sweep one hour. That pays your debt. I'll hep you pay it. I'll ast 'm and see if he won't let me hep you."

"I'm going to cancel the debt," says Professor Herbert. "I just wanted you to understand, Luster."

"I understand," says Pa, "and since I understand he must pay his debt fer th' tree and I'm goin' to help 'im."

"Don't do that," says Professor Herbert. "It's all on me."

"We don't do things like that," says Pa, "we're just and honest people. We don't want somethin' for nothin'. Professor Herbert, you're wrong now and I'm right. You'll haf to listen to me. I've larned a lot from you. My boy must go on. Th' world has left me. It changed while I've raised my family and ploughed th' hills. I'm a just and honest man. I don't skip debts. I ain't larned 'em to do that. I ain't got much larnin' myself but I do know right from wrong atter I see through a thing."

Professor Herbert went home. Pa and I stayed and swept one hour. It looked funny to see Pa use a broom. He never used one at home. Mom used the broom. Pa used the plough. Pa did hard work. Pa says: "I can't sweep. Look at th' streaks o' dirt I leave on th' floor! I'll jist do th' best I can, Dave. I've been wrong about th' school."

I says: "Did you know Professor Herbert can get a warrant out for you for bringing your pistol to school and showing it in his office? They can railroad you for that!"

"That's all made right," says Pa. "I've made that right. Professor Herbert ain't goin' to take it to court. He likes me. I like 'im. We jist had to get together. He had the remedies. He showed me. You must go on to school. I am as strong a man as ever come out'n th' hills fer my years and th' hard work I've done. But I'm behind, Dave. I'm a little man. Your hands will be softer than mine. Your clothes will be better. You'll allus look cleaner than your old Pap. Jist remember Dave to pay your debts and be honest. Jist be kind to animals and don't bother th' snakes. That's all I got agin th' school. Puttin' black snakes to sleep and cuttin' 'em open."

It was late when we got home. Stars were in the sky. The moon was up. The ground was frozen. Pa took his time going home. I couldn't run like I did the night before. It was ten o'clock before we got the work finished, our suppers eaten. Pa sat before the fire and told Mom he was going to take her and show her a germ some time. Mom hadn't seen one either. Pa told her about the high school and the fine man Professor Herbert was. He told Mom about the strange school across the hill and how different it was from the school in their day and time.

Speaking about Professor Herbert, Pa says, "We jist had to get together." What did that involve?

Thank You, M'am

Langston Hughes

She was a large woman with a large purse that had everything in it but a hammer and nails. It had a long strap, and she carried it slung across her shoulder. It was about eleven o'clock at night, dark, and she was walking alone, when a boy ran up behind her and tried to snatch her purse. The strap broke with the sudden single tug the boy gave it from behind. But the boy's weight and the weight of the purse combined caused him to lose his balance. Instead of taking off full blast as he had hoped, the boy fell on his back on the sidewalk and his legs flew up. The large woman simply turned around and kicked him right square in his blue-jeaned sitter. Then she reached down, picked the boy up by his shirtfront, and shook him until his teeth rattled.

After that the woman said, "Pick up my pocketbook, boy, and give it here."

She still held him tightly. But she bent down enough to permit him to stoop and pick up her purse. Then she said, "Now ain't you ashamed of yourself?"

Firmly gripped by his shirtfront, the boy said, "Yes'm."

The woman said, "What did you want to do it for?"

The boy said, "I didn't aim to."

She said, "You lie!"

By that time two or three people passed, stopped, turned to look, and some stood watching.

"If I turn you loose, will you run?" asked the woman.

"Yes'm," said the boy.

"Then I won't turn you loose," said the woman. She did not release him.

"Lady, I'm sorry," whispered the boy.

"Um-hum! Your face is dirty. I got a great mind to wash your face for you. Ain't you got nobody home to tell you to wash your face?"

"No'm," said the boy.

"Then it will get washed this evening," said the large woman, starting up the street, dragging the frightened boy behind her.

He looked as if he were fourteen or fifteen, frail and willow-wild, in tennis shoes and blue jeans.

The woman said, "You ought to be my son. I would teach you right from wrong. Least I can do right now is to wash your face. Are you hungry?"

"No'm," said the being-dragged boy. "I just want you to turn me loose."

"Was I bothering *you* when I turned the corner?" asked the woman.

"No'm."

"But you put yourself in contact with *me,*" said the woman. "If you think that that contact is not going to last a while, you got another thought coming. When I get through with you, sir, you are going to remember Mrs. Luella Bates Washington Jones."

Sweat popped out on the boy's face, and he began to struggle. Mrs. Jones stopped, jerked him around in front of her, put a half nelson about his neck, and continued to drag him up the street. When she got to her door, she dragged the boy inside, down a hall, and into a large kitchenette-furnished room at the rear of the house. She switched on the light and left the door open. The boy could hear other roomers laughing and talking in the large house. Some of their doors were open, too, so he knew he and the woman were not alone. The woman still had him by the neck in the middle of her room.

She said, "What is your name?"

"Roger," answered the boy.

"Then, Roger, you go to that sink and wash your face," said the woman, whereupon she turned him loose—at last. Roger looked at the door—looked at the woman—looked at the door—*and went to the sink.*

"Let the water run until it gets warm," she said. "Here's a clean towel."

"You gonna take me to jail?" asked the boy, bending over the sink.

"Not with that face, I would not take you nowhere," said the woman. "Here I am trying to get home to cook me a bite to eat, and you snatch my pocketbook! Maybe you ain't been to your supper either, late as it be. Have you?"

"There's nobody home at my house," said the boy.

"Then we'll eat," said the woman. "I believe you're hungry—or been hungry—to try to snatch my pocketbook!"

"I want a pair of blue suede shoes," said the boy.

"Well, you didn't have to snatch *my* pocketbook to get some suede shoes," said Mrs. Luella Bates Washington Jones. "You could of asked me."

"M'am?"

The water dripping from his face, the boy looked at her. There was a long pause. A very long pause. After he had dried his face and not knowing what else to do, dried it again, the boy turned around, wondering what next. The door was open. He could make a dash for it down the hall. He could run, run, *run!*

The woman was sitting on the daybed. After a while she said, "I were young once and I wanted things I could not get."

There was another long pause. The boy's mouth opened. Then he frowned, not knowing he frowned.

The woman said, "Um-hum! You thought I was going

to say *but*, didn't you? You thought I was going to say, *but I didn't snatch people's pocketbooks*. Well, I wasn't going to say that." Pause. Silence. "I have done things, too, which I would not tell you, son—neither tell God, if He didn't already know. Everybody's got something in common. So you set down while I fix us something to eat. You might run that comb through your hair so you will look presentable."

In another corner of the room behind a screen was a gas plate and an icebox. Mrs. Jones got up and went behind the screen. The woman did not watch the boy to see if he was going to run now, nor did she watch her purse, which she left behind her on the daybed. But the boy took care to sit on the far side of the room, away from the purse, where he thought she could easily see him out of the corner of her eye if she wanted to. He did not trust the woman *not* to trust him. And he did not want to be mistrusted now.

"Do you need somebody to go to the store," asked the boy, "maybe to get some milk or something?"

"Don't believe I do," said the woman, "unless you just want sweet milk yourself. I was going to make cocoa out of this canned milk I got here."

"That will be fine," said the boy.

She heated some lima beans and ham she had in the icebox, made the cocoa, and set the table. The woman did not ask the boy anything about where he lived, or his folks, or anything else that would embarrass him. Instead, as they ate, she told him about her job in a hotel beauty shop that stayed open late, what the work was like, and how all kinds of women came in and out, blondes, redheads, and Spanish. Then she cut him a half of her ten-cent cake.

"Eat some more, son," she said.

When they finished eating, she got up and said, "Now

here, take this ten dollars and buy yourself some blue suede shoes. And next time, do not make the mistake of latching onto *my* pocketbook *nor nobody else's*—because shoes got by devilish ways will burn your feet. I got to get my rest now. But from here on in, son, I hope you will behave yourself."

She led the way down the hall to the front door and opened it. "Good night! Behave yourself, boy!" she said, looking out into the street as he went down the steps.

The boy wanted to say something other than, "Thank you, m'am," to Mrs. Luella Bates Washington Jones, but although his lips moved, he couldn't even say that as he turned at the foot of the barren stoop and looked up at the large woman in the door. Then she shut the door.

Why do you think the boy said "Thank you, m'am." Just relief? Glad he wasn't turned in? Because he liked the lady?

We Are But a Moment's Sunlight

Some will come and some will go
And we shall surely pass
When the one who left us here
Returns for us at last;
We are but a moment's sunlight
Fading on the grass.
C'mon people now—smile on your brother
Hey let's get together
And love one another right now.

Chet Powers

David and Jonathan

(from 1 Samuel 18, 19, and 20)

1 When he had finished speaking to Saul, the soul of Jonathan was knit to the soul of David, and Jonathan loved him as his own soul. 2 And Saul took him that day, and would not let him return to his father's house. 3 Then Jonathan made a covenant with David, because he loved him as his own soul. 4 And Jonathan stripped himself of the robe that was upon him, and gave it to David, and his armor, and even his sword and his bow and his girdle. 5 And David went out and was successful wherever Saul sent him; so that Saul set him over the men of war. And this was good in the sight of all the people and also in the sight of Saul's servants.

6 As they were coming home, when David returned from slaying the Philistine, the women came out of all the cities of Israel, singing and dancing, to meet King Saul, with timbrels, with songs of joy, and with instruments of music. 7 And the women sang to one another as they made merry,

"Saul has slain his thousands,
and David his ten thousands."

8 And Saul was very angry, and this saying displeased him; he said, "They have ascribed to David ten thousands, and to me they have ascribed thousands; and what more can he have but the kingdom?" 9 And Saul eyed David from that day on.

(Saul assigns David to a difficult battle hoping to have him killed. The plan fails as David wins the battle.)

1 And Saul spoke to Jonathan his son and to all his servants, that they should kill David. But Jonathan,

Saul's son, delighted much in David. 2 And Jonathan
told David, "Saul my father seeks to kill you; therefore
take heed to yourself in the morning, stay in a secret
place and hide yourself; 3 and I will go out and stand
beside my father in the field where you are, and I will
speak to my father about you; and if I learn anything I
will tell you." 4 And Jonathan spoke well of David to
Saul his father, and said to him, "Let not the king sin
against his servant David; because he has not sinned
against you, and because his deeds have been of good
service to you; 5 for he took his life in his hand and he
slew the Philistine, and the LORD wrought a great victory
for all Israel. You saw it, and rejoiced; why then will
you sin against innocent blood by killing David without
cause?" 6 And Saul hearkened to the voice of Jonathan;
Saul swore, "As the LORD lives, he shall not be put to
death." 7 And Jonathan called David, and Jonathan
showed him all these things. And Jonathan brought
David to Saul, and he was in his presence as before.

8 And there was war again; and David went out and
fought with the Philistines, and made a great slaughter
among them, so that they fled before him. 9 Then an evil
spirit from the LORD came upon Saul, as he sat in his
house with his spear in his hand; and David was playing
the lyre. 10 And Saul sought to pin David to the wall
with the spear; but he eluded Saul, so that he struck the
spear into the wall. And David fled, and escaped.

* * * * *

1 Then David fled from Naioth in Ramah, and came
and said before Jonathan, "What have I done? What is
my guilt? And what is my sin before your father, that
he seeks my life?" 2 And he said to him, "Far from it!
You shall not die. Behold, my father does nothing either

great or small without disclosing it to me; and why
should my father hide this from me? It is not so." [3] But
David replied, "Your father knows well that I have
found favor in your eyes; and he thinks, 'Let not Jonathan know this, lest he be grieved.' But truly, as the
LORD lives and as your soul lives, there is but a step
between me and death." [4] Then said Jonathan to David,
"Whatever you say, I will do for you." [5] David said to
Jonathan, "Behold, tomorrow is the new moon, and I
should not fail to sit at table with the king; but let me
go, that I may hide myself in the field till the third day
at evening. [6] If your father misses me at all, then say,
'David earnestly asked leave of me to run to Bethlehem
his city; for there is a yearly sacrifice there for all the
family.' [7] If he says, 'Good!' it will be well with your
servant; but if he is angry, then know that evil is
determined by him. [8] Therefore deal kindly with your
servant, for you have brought your servant into a sacred
covenant with you. But if there is guilt in me, slay me
yourself; for why should you bring me to your father?"
[9] And Jonathan said, "Far be it from you! If I knew that
it was determined by my father that evil should come
upon you, would I not tell you?" [10] Then said David to
Jonathan, "Who will tell me if your father answers you
roughly?" [11] And Jonathan said to David, "Come, let us
go out into the field." So they both went out into the
field.

[12] And Jonathan said to David, "The LORD, the God
of Israel, be witness! When I have sounded my father,
about this time tomorrow, or the third day, behold, if
he is well disposed toward David, shall I not then send
and disclose it to you? [13] But should it please my father
to do you harm, the LORD do so to Jonathan, and
more also, if I do not disclose it to you, and send you
away, that you may go in safety. May the LORD be

with you, as he has been with my father. 14 If I am still alive, show me the loyal love of the LORD, that I may not die; 15 and do not cut off your loyalty from my house for ever. When the LORD cuts off every one of the enemies of David from the face of the earth, 16 let not the name of Jonathan be cut off from the house of David. And may the LORD take vengeance on David's enemies." 17 And Jonathan made David swear again by his love for him; for he loved him as he loved his own soul.

18 Then Jonathan said to him, "Tomorrow is the new moon; and you will be missed, because your seat will be empty. 19 And on the third day you will be greatly missed; then go to the place where you hid yourself when the matter was in hand, and remain beside yonder stone heap. 20 And I will shoot three arrows to the side of it, as though I shot at a mark. 21 And behold, I will send the lad, saying, 'Go, find the arrows.' If I say to the lad, 'Look, the arrows are on this side of you, take them,' then you are to come, for, as the LORD lives, it is safe for you and there is no danger. 22 But if I say to the youth, 'Look, the arrows are beyond you,' then go; for the LORD has sent you away. 23 And as for the matter of which you and I have spoken, behold, the LORD is between you and me for ever."

24 So David hid himself in the field; and when the new moon came, the king sat down to eat food. 25 The king sat upon his seat, as at other times, upon the seat by the wall; Jonathan sat opposite, and Abner sat by Saul's side, but David's place was empty.

26 Yet Saul did not say anything that day; for he thought, "Something has befallen him; he is not clean, surely he is not clean." 27 But on the second day, the morrow after the new moon, David's place was empty. And Saul said to Jonathan his son, "Why has not the

son of Jesse come to the meal, either yesterday or
today?" [28]Jonathan answered Saul, "David earnestly
asked leave of me to go to Bethlehem; [29]he said, 'Let
me go; for our family holds a sacrifice in the city, and
my brother has commanded me to be there. So now, if I
have found favor in your eyes, let me get away, and see
my brothers.' For this reason he has not come to the
king's table."

[30]Then Saul's anger was kindled against Jonathan,
and he said to him, "You son of a perverse, rebellious
woman, do I not know that you have chosen the son of
Jesse to your own shame, and to the shame of your
mother's nakedness? [31]For as long as the son of Jesse
lives upon the earth, neither you nor your kingdom shall
be established. Therefore send and fetch him to me, for
he shall surely die." [32]Then Jonathan answered Saul his
father, "Why should he be put to death? What has he
done?" [33]But Saul cast his spear at him to smite him; so
Jonathan knew that his father was determined to put
David to death. [34]And Jonathan rose from the table in
fierce anger and ate no food the second day of the
month, for he was grieved for David, because his father
had disgraced him.

[35]In the morning Jonathan went out into the field to
the appointment with David, and with him a little lad.
[36]And he said to his lad, "Run and find the arrows
which I shoot." As the lad ran, he shot an arrow beyond
him. [37]And when the lad came to the place of the
arrow which Jonathan had shot, Jonathan called after
the lad and said, "Is not the arrow beyond you?"
[38]And Jonathan called after the lad, "Hurry, make
haste, stay not." So Jonathan's lad gathered up the
arrows, and came to his master. [39]But the lad knew
nothing; only Jonathan and David knew the matter.
[40]And Jonathan gave his weapons to his lad, and said to

him, "Go and carry them to the city." 41 And as soon as
the lad had gone, David rose from beside the stone heap
and fell on his face to the ground, and bowed three
times; and they kissed one another, and wept with one
another, until David recovered himself. 42 Then Jonathan said to David, "Go in peace, forasmuch as we have
sworn both of us in the name of the LORD, saying, 'The
LORD shall be between me and you, and between my
descendants and your descendants, for ever.' " And he
rose and departed; and Jonathan went into the city.

The Revised Standard Version

Loving someone sometimes takes courage and self-sacrifice. How is that true of Jonathan? Who sacrificed most for the friendship, David or Jonathan?

The Oyster and the Pearl

William Saroyan

Characters

Harry Van Dusen, *a barber*
Clay Larrabee, *a boy on Saturday*
Vivian McCutcheon, *a new schoolteacher*
Clark Larrabee, *Clay's father*
Man, *a writer*
Roxanna Larrabee, *Clay's sister*
Greeley, *Clay's pal*
Judge Applegarth, *a beachcomber*
Wozzeck, *a watch repairer*
Attendant, *a man from the gasoline station*

Scene: HARRY VAN DUSEN'S *barber shop in O.K.-by-the-Sea, California, population 909. The sign on* *the window says:* Harry Van Dusen, Barber. *It's an old-fashioned shop, crowded with stuff not usually found in barber shops . . .* HARRY *himself, for instance. He has never been known to put on a barber's white jacket or to work without a hat of some sort on his head: a stovepipe, a derby, a western, a homburg, a skullcap, a beret, or a straw, as if putting on these various hats somewhat expressed the quality of his soul or suggested the range of it.*

On the walls, on shelves, are many odds and ends, some apparently washed up by the sea, which is a block down the street: abalone and other shells, rocks, pieces of driftwood, a life jacket, rope, sea plants. There is one old-fashioned chair.

When the play begins, HARRY *is seated in the chair. A boy of nine or ten named* CLAY LARRABEE *is giving him a haircut.* HARRY *is reading a book, one of many in the shop.*

Clay: Well, I did what you told me, Mr. Van Dusen. I hope it's all right. I'm no barber, though. *(He begins to comb the hair.)*

Harry: You just gave me a haircut, didn't you?

Clay: I don't know *what* you'd call it. You want to look at it in the mirror? *(He holds out a small mirror.)*

Harry: No, thanks. I remember the last one.

Clay: I guess I'll never be a barber.

Harry: Maybe not. On the other hand, you may turn out to be the one man hidden away in the junk of the world who will bring merriment to the tired old human heart.

Clay: Who? Me?

Harry: Why not?

Clay: Merriment to the tired old human heart? How do you do that?

Harry: Compose a symphony, paint a picture, write a book, invent a philosophy.

Clay: Not me! Did you ever do stuff like that?

Harry: I did.

Clay: What did you do?

Harry: Invented a philosophy.

Clay: What's that?

Harry: A way to live.

Clay: What way did you invent?

Harry: The *Take-it-easy way.*

Clay: That sounds pretty good.

Harry: All philosophies *sound* good. The trouble with mine was, I kept forgetting to take it easy. Until one day. The day I came off the highway into this barber shop. The barber told me the shop was for sale. I told him all I had to my name was eighty dollars. He sold me the shop for seventy-five and threw in the haircut. I've been here ever since. That was twenty-four years ago.

Clay: Before I was born.

Harry: Fifteen or sixteen years before you were born.

Clay: How old were you then?

Harry: Old enough to know a good thing when I saw it.

Clay: What did you see?

Harry: O.K.-by-the-Sea, and this shop—the proper place for me to stop. That's a couplet. Shakespeare had them at the end of a scene, so I guess that's the end of this haircut. *(He gets out of the chair, goes to the hat tree, and puts on a derby.)*

Clay: I guess I'd never get a haircut if you weren't in town, Mr. Van Dusen.

Harry: Nobody would, since I'm the only barber.

Clay: I mean, free of charge.

Harry: I give you a haircut free of charge, you give me a haircut free of charge. That's fair and square.

Clay: Yes, but you're a barber. You get a dollar a haircut.

Harry: Now and then I do. Now and then I don't.

Clay: Well, anyhow, thanks a lot. I guess I'll go down to the beach now and look for stuff.

Harry: I'd go with you, but I'm expecting a little Saturday business.

Clay: This time I'm going to find something *real good*, I think.

Harry: The sea washes up some pretty good things at that, doesn't it?

Clay: It sure does, except money.

Harry: What do you want with money?

Clay: Things I need.

Harry: What do you need?

Clay: I want to get my father to come home again. I want to buy Mother a present. . . .

Harry: Now, wait a minute, Clay; let me get this straight. Where *is* your father?

Clay: I don't know. He went off the day after I got my last haircut, about a month ago.

Harry: What do you mean, he went off?

Clay: He just picked up and went off.

Harry: Did he say when he was coming back?

Clay: No. All he said was, "Enough's enough." He wrote it on the kitchen wall.

Harry: Enough's enough?

Clay: Yeah. We all thought he'd be back in a day or two, but now we know we've got to *find* him and *bring* him back.

Harry: How do you expect to do that?

Clay: Well, we put an ad in *The O.K.-by-the-Sea Gull* . . . that comes out every Saturday.

Harry *(opening the paper)*: This paper? But your

father's not in town. How will he see an ad in this paper?

Clay: He *might* see it. Anyhow, we don't know what else to do. We're living off the money we saved from the summer we worked, but there ain't much left.

Harry: The summer you worked?

Clay: Yeah. Summer before last, just before we moved here, we picked cotton in Kern County. My father, my mother, and me.

Harry *(indicating the paper)*: What do you say in your ad?

Clay *(looking at it)*: Well, I say . . . Clark Larrabee. Come home. Your fishing tackle's in the closet safe and sound. The fishing's good, plenty of cabezon, perch, and bass. Let bygones be bygones. We miss you. Mama, Clay, Roxanna, Rufus, Clara.

Harry: That's a good ad.

Clay: Do you think if my father reads it, he'll come home?

Harry: I don't know, Clay. I hope so.

Clay: Yeah. Thanks a lot for the haircut, Mr. Van Dusen.

(CLAY *goes out.* HARRY *takes off the derby, lathers his face, and begins to shave with a straight-edge razor. A pretty girl in a swimming suit comes into the shop, closing a colorful parasol. She has long blonde hair.)*

Harry: Miss America, I presume.

The girl: Miss McCutcheon.

Harry: Harry Van Dusen.

The girl: How do you do.

Harry *(bowing)*: Miss McCutcheon.

The girl: I'm new here.

Harry: You'd be new anywhere—brand-new, I might say. Surely you don't live here?

The girl: As a matter of fact, I do. At any rate, I've been here since last Sunday. You see, I'm the new teacher at the school.

Harry: You are?

The girl: Yes, I am.

Harry: How do you like it?

The girl: One week at this school has knocked me for a loop. As a matter of fact, I want to quit and go home to San Francisco. At the same time I have a feeling I ought to stay. What do you think?

Harry: Are you serious? I mean, in asking me?

The girl: Of course I'm serious. You've been here a long time. You know everybody in town. Shall I go, or shall I stay?

Harry: Depends on what you're looking for. I stopped here twenty-four years ago because I decided I wasn't looking for anything any more. Well, I was mistaken. I *was* looking, and I've found exactly what I was looking for.

The girl: What's that?

Harry: A chance to take my time. That's why I'm still here. What are *you* looking for, Miss McCutcheon?

The girl: Well. . . .

Harry: I mean, besides a husband. . . .

The girl: I'm not looking for a husband. I expect a husband to look for me.

Harry: That's fair.

The girl: I'm looking for a chance to teach.

Harry: That's fair too.

The girl: But this town! . . . The children just don't seem to care about anything—whether they get good grades or bad, whether they pass or fail, or anything else. On top of that, almost all of them are unruly.

The only thing they seem to be interested in is games, and the sea. That's why I'm on my way to the beach now. I thought if I could watch them on a Saturday, I might understand them better.

Harry: Yes, that's a thought.

The girl: Nobody seems to have any sensible ambition. It's all fun and play. How can I teach children like that? What can I teach them?

Harry: English.

The girl: Of course.

Harry *(drying his face)*: Singing, dancing, cooking. . . .

The girl: Cooking? . . . I must say I expected to see a much older man.

Harry: Well! Thank you!

The girl: Not at all.

Harry: The question is, Shall you stay, or shall you go back to San Francisco?

The girl: Yes.

Harry: The answer is, Go back while the going's good.

The girl: Why? I mean, a moment ago I believed you were going to point out why I ought to stay, and then suddenly you say I ought to go back. Why?

Harry *(after a pause)*: You're too good for a town like this.

The girl: I am not!

Harry: Too young and too intelligent. Youth and intelligence need excitement.

The girl: There are *kinds* of excitement.

Harry: Yes, there are. You need the big-city kind. There isn't an eligible bachelor in town.

The girl: You seem to think all I want is to find a husband.

Harry: But only to teach. You want to teach him to become a father, so you can have a lot of children of your own—to teach.

The girl: *(She sits almost angrily in the chair and speaks very softly.)* I'd like a poodle haircut if you don't mind, Mr. Van Dusen.

Harry: You'll have to get that in San Francisco, I'm afraid.

The girl: Why? Aren't you a barber?

Harry: I am.

The girl: Well, this is your shop. It's open for business. I'm a customer. I've got money. I want a poodle haircut.

Harry: I don't know how to give a poodle haircut, but even if I knew how, I wouldn't do it.

The girl: Why not?

Harry: I don't give women haircuts. The only women who visit this shop bring their small children for haircuts.

The girl: I want a poodle haircut, Mr. Van Dusen.

Harry: I'm sorry, Miss McCutcheon. In my sleep, in a nightmare, I would *not* cut your hair.

(The sound of a truck stopping is heard from across the street.)

The girl *(softly, patiently, but firmly):* Mr. Van Dusen, I've decided to stay, and the first thing I've got to do is change my appearance. I don't fit into the scenery around here.

Harry: Oh, I don't know—if I were a small boy going to school, I'd say you look just right.

The girl: You're just like the children. They don't take me seriously, either. They think I'm nothing more than a pretty girl who is going to give up in despair and go home. If you give me a poodle haircut, I'll look more—well, plain and simple. I plan to dress differently, too. I'm determined to teach here.

You've got to help me. Now, Mr. Van Dusen, the shears, please.

Harry: I'm sorry, Miss McCutcheon. There's no need to change your *appearance* at all.

(CLARK LARRABEE *comes into the shop.)*

Harry: You're next, Clark. (HARRY *helps* MISS McCUTCHEON *out of the chair. She gives him an angry glance.)*

The girl *(whispering):* I won't forget this rudeness, Mr. Van Dusen.

Harry *(also whispering):* Never whisper in O.K.-by-the-Sea. People misunderstand. *(Loudly.)* Good day, Miss.

(MISS McCUTCHEON *opens her parasol with anger and leaves the shop.* CLARK LARRABEE *has scarcely noticed her. He stands looking at* HARRY'S *junk on the shelves.)*

Harry: Well, Clark, I haven't seen you in a long time.

Clark: I'm just passing through, Harry. Thought I might run into Clay here.

Harry: He was here a little while ago.

Clark: How is he?

Harry: He's fine, Clark.

Clark: I been working in Salinas. Got a ride down in a truck. It's across the street now at the gasoline station.

Harry: You've been home, of course?

Clark: No, I haven't.

Harry: Oh?

Clark *(after a slight pause):* I've left Fay, Harry.

Harry: You got time for a haircut, Clark?

Clark: No, thanks, Harry. I've got to go back to Salinas on that truck across the street.

Harry: Clay's somewhere on the beach.

Clark *(handing* HARRY *three ten-dollar bills):* Give him this, will you? Thirty dollars. Don't tell him I gave it to you.

Harry: Why not?

Clark: I'd rather he didn't know I was around. Is he all right?

Harry: Sure, Clark. They're *all* O.K. I mean. . . .

Clark: Tell him to take the money home to his mother. *(He picks up the newspaper,* The Gull.)

Harry: Sure, Clark. It came out this morning. Take it along.

Clark: Thanks. *(He puts the paper in his pocket.)* How've things been going with *you*, Harry?

Harry: Oh, I can't kick. Two or three haircuts a day. A lot of time to read. A few laughs. A few surprises. The sea. The fishing. It's a good life.

Clark: Keep an eye on Clay, will you? I mean—well, I *had* to do it.

Harry: Sure.

Clark: Yeah, well. . . . That's the first money I've been able to save. When I make some more, I'd like to send it here, so you can hand it to Clay, to take home.

Harry: Anything you say, Clark.

(There is the sound of the truck's horn blowing.)

Clark: Well. . . . *(He goes to the door.)* Thanks, Harry; thanks a lot.

Harry: Good seeing you, Clark.

(CLARK LARRABEE *goes out.* HARRY *watches him. A truck shifting gears is heard, and then the sound of the truck driving off.* HARRY *picks up a book, changes hats, sits down in the chair, and begins to read. A* MAN *of forty or so, well-dressed, rather swift, comes in.)*

The man: Where's the barber?

Harry: I'm the barber.

The man: Can I get a haircut, real quick?

Harry *(getting out of the chair):* Depends on what you mean by real quick.

The man *(sitting down):* Well, just a haircut then.

Harry *(putting an apron around the* MAN): O.K. I don't believe I've seen you before.

The man: No. They're changing the oil in my car across the street. Thought I'd step in here and get a haircut. Get it out of the way before I get to Hollywood. How many miles is it?

Harry: About two hundred straight down the highway. You can't miss it.

The man: What town is *this?*

Harry: O.K.-by-the-Sea.

The man: What do the people do here?

Harry: Well, I cut hair. Friend of mine named Wozzeck repairs watches, radios, alarm clocks, and sells jewelry.

The man: Who does he sell it to?

Harry: The people here. It's imitation stuff mainly.

The man: Factory here? Farms? Fishing?

Harry: No. Just the few stores on the highway, the houses further back in the hills, the church, and the school. You a salesman?

The man: No, I'm a writer.

Harry: What do you write?

The man: A little bit of everything. How about the haircut?

Harry: You got to be in Hollywood tonight?

The man: I don't have to be anywhere tonight, but that was the idea. Why?

Harry: Well, I've always said a writer could step into a place like this, watch things a little while, and get a whole book out of it, or a play.

The man: Or if he was a poet, a sonnet.

Harry: Do you like Shakespeare's?

The man: They're just about the best in English.

Harry: It's not often I get a writer in here. As a matter of fact, you're the only writer I've had in here in twenty years, not counting Fenton.

The man: Who's he?

Harry: Fenton Lockhart.

The man: What's he write?

Harry: He gets out the weekly paper. Writes the whole thing himself.

The man: Yeah. Well. . . . How about the haircut?

Harry: O.K.

(HARRY *puts a hot towel around the man's head.* MISS McCUTCHEON, *carrying a cane chair without one leg and without a seat, comes in. With her is* CLAY *with something in his hand, a smaller boy named* GREELEY *with a bottle of sea water, and* ROXANNA *with an assortment of shells.)*

Clay: I got an oyster here, Mr. Van Dusen.

Greeley: Miss McCutcheon claims there *ain't* a big pearl in it.

Harry *(looking at* MISS McCUTCHEON): Is she willing to admit there's a *little* one in it?

Greeley: I don't know. I know I got sea water in this bottle.

Miss McCutcheon: Mr. Van Dusen, Clay Larrabee seems to believe there's a pearl in this oyster he happens to have found on the beach.

Clay: I didn't *happen* to find it. I went looking for it. You know Black Rock, Mr. Van Dusen? Well, the tide hardly ever gets low enough for a fellow to get around to the ocean side of Black Rock, but a little while ago it did, so I went around there to that side. I got to poking around, and I found this oyster.

Harry: I've been here twenty-four years, Clay, and this is the first time I've ever heard of anybody finding an oyster on our beach—at Black Rock or anywhere else.

Clay: Well, *I* did, Mr. Van Dusen. It's shut tight, it's alive, and there's a pearl in it, worth at least three hundred dollars.

Greeley: A *big* pearl.

Miss McCutcheon: Now, you children listen to me. It's never too soon for any of us to face the truth, which is supposed to set us free, not imprison us. The truth is, Clay, you want money because you need money. The truth is also that you have found an oyster. The truth is also that there is no pearl in the oyster.

Greeley: How do you know? Did you look?

Miss McCutcheon: No, but neither did Clay, and inasmuch as only one oyster in a million has a pearl in it, truth favors the probability that this is not the millionth oyster . . . the oyster with the pearl in it.

Clay: There's a *big* pearl in the oyster.

Miss McCutcheon: Mr. Van Dusen, shall we open the oyster and show Clay and his sister Roxanna and their friend Greeley that there is no pearl in it?

Harry: In a moment, Miss McCutcheon. And what's that *you* have?

Miss McCutcheon: A chair, as you see.

Harry: How many legs does it have?

Miss McCutcheon: Three, of course. I can count to three, I hope.

Harry: What do you want with a chair with only three legs?

Miss McCutcheon: I'm going to bring things from the sea the same as everybody else in town.

Harry: But everybody else in town *doesn't* bring things from the sea—just the children, Judge Applegarth, Fenton Lockhart, and myself.

Miss McCutcheon: In any case, the same as the children, Judge Applegarth, Fenton Lockhart, and you. Judge Applegarth? Who's he?

Harry: He judged swine at a county fair one time, so we call him Judge.

Miss McCutcheon: Pigs?

Harry: Swine's a little old-fashioned, but I prefer it to pigs, and since both words mean the same thing—Well, I wouldn't care to call a man like Arthur Applegarth a pig judge.

Miss McCutcheon: Did he actually judge swine, as you prefer to put it, at a county fair, one time? Did he even do *that?*

Harry: Nobody checked up. He *said* he did.

Miss McCutcheon: So that entitled him to be called Judge Applegarth?

Harry: It certainly did.

Miss McCutcheon: On that basis, Clay's oyster has a big pearl in it because he *says* so, is that it?

Harry: I didn't say that.

Miss McCutcheon: Are we living in the Middle Ages, Mr. Van Dusen?

Greeley: No, this is 1953, Miss McCutcheon.

Miss McCutcheon: Yes, Greeley, and to illustrate what I mean, that's water you have in that bottle. Nothing else.

Greeley: *Sea* water.

Miss McCutcheon: Yes, but there's nothing else in the bottle.

Greeley: No, but there's little things in the water. You can't see them now, but they'll show up later. The water of the sea is full of things.

Miss McCutcheon: Salt, perhaps.

Greeley: No. *Living* things. If I look hard, I can see some of them now.

Miss McCutcheon: You can *imagine* seeing them. Mr. Van Dusen, are you going to help me or not?

Harry: What do you want me to do?

Miss McCutcheon: Open the oyster, of course, so Clay will see for himself that there's no pearl in it. So he'll begin to face reality, as he should, as each of us should.

Harry: Clay, do you mind if I look at the oyster a minute?

Clay *(handing the oyster to* HARRY): There's a big pearl in it, Mr. Van Dusen.

Harry *(examining the oyster):* Clay . . . Roxanna . . . Greeley . . . I wonder if you'd go down the street to Wozzeck's. Tell him to come here the first chance he gets. I'd rather he opened this oyster. I might damage the pearl.

Clay, Greeley, *and* **Roxanna**: O.K., Mr. Van Dusen.

(They go out.)

Miss McCutcheon: What pearl? What in the world do you think you're trying to do to the minds of these children? How am I ever going to teach them the principles of truth with an influence like yours to fight against?

Harry: Miss McCutcheon. The people of O.K.-by-the-Sea

are all poor. Most of them can't afford to pay for the haircuts I give them. There's no excuse for this town at all, but the sea is here, and so are the hills. A few people find jobs a couple of months every year North or South, come back half dead of homesickness, and live on next to nothing the rest of the year. A few get pensions. Every family has a garden and a few chickens, and they make a few dollars selling vegetables and eggs. In a town of almost a thousand people there isn't one rich man. Not even one who is well-off. And yet these people are the richest I have ever known. Clay doesn't really want money, as you seem to think. He wants his father to come home, and he thinks money will help get his father home. As a matter of fact, his father is the man who stepped in here just as you were leaving. He left thirty dollars for me to give to Clay, to take home. His father and his mother haven't been getting along. Clark Larrabee's a fine man. He's not the town drunk or anything like that, but having four kids to provide for he gets to feeling ashamed of the showing he's making, and he starts drinking. He wants his kids to live in a good house of their own, wear good clothes, and all the other things fathers have always wanted for their kids. His wife wants these things for the kids too. They don't have these things, so they fight. They had one too many fights about a month ago, so Clark went off—he's working in Salinas. He's either going to keep moving away from his family, or he's going to come back. It all depends on—well, I don't know what. This oyster maybe. Clay maybe. *(Softly.)* You and me maybe.

(There is a pause. He looks at the oyster. MISS McCUTCHEON *looks at it too.)*

Harry: Clay believes there's a pearl in this oyster for the same reason you and I believe whatever *we* believe to keep *us* going.

Miss McCutcheon: Are you suggesting we play a trick on Clay, in order to carry out your mumbo-jumbo ideas?

Harry: Well, maybe it *is* a trick. I know Wozzeck's got a few pretty good-sized cultivated pearls.

Miss McCutcheon: You plan to have Wozzeck pretend he has found a pearl in the oyster when he opens it, is that it?

Harry: I plan to get three hundred dollars to Clay.

Miss McCutcheon: Do you *have* three hundred dollars?

Harry: Not quite.

Miss McCutcheon: What about the other children who need money? Do you plan to put pearls in oysters for them, too? Not just here in O.K.-by-the-Sea. Everywhere. This isn't the only town in the world where people are poor, where fathers and mothers fight, where families break up.

Harry: No, it isn't, but it's the only town where I live.

Miss McCutcheon: I give up. What do you want me to do?

Harry: Well, could you find it in your heart to be just a little less sure about things when you talk to the kids—I mean, the troubled ones? You can get Clay around to the truth easy enough just as soon as he gets his father home.

(ARTHUR APPLEGARTH *comes in.)*

Harry: Judge Applegarth, may I present Miss McCutcheon?

The Judge *(removing his hat and bowing low):* An honor, Miss.

Miss McCutcheon: How do you do, Judge.

Harry: Miss McCutcheon's the new teacher at the school.

The Judge: We are honored to have you. The children, the parents, and—the rest of us.

Miss McCutcheon: Thank you, Judge. *(To* HARRY, *whispering.)* I'll be back as soon as I change my clothes.

Harry *(whispering):* I told you not to whisper.

Miss McCutcheon *(whispering):* I shall expect you to give me a poodle haircut.

Harry *(whispering):* Are you out of your mind?

Miss McCutcheon *(aloud):* Good day, Judge.

The Judge *(bowing):* Good day, Miss. *(While he is bent over, he takes a good look at her knees, calves, ankles, and bow-tied sandals.)*

(MISS McCUTCHEON *goes out.* JUDGE APPLEGARTH *looks from the door to* HARRY.)

The Judge: She won't last a month.

Harry: Why not?

The Judge: Too pretty. Our school needs an old battle-ax, like the teachers we had when we went to school, not a bathing beauty. Well, Harry, what's new?

Harry: Just the teacher, I guess.

The Judge: You know, Harry, the beach isn't what it used to be—not at all. I don't mind the competition we're getting from the kids. It's just that the quality of the stuff the sea's washing up isn't good any more. *(Goes to door.)*

Harry: I don't know. Clay Larrabee found an oyster this morning.

The Judge: He did? Well, one oyster don't make a stew, Harry. On my way home I'll drop in and let you see what I find.

Harry: O.K., Judge.

(The JUDGE *goes out.* HARRY *comes to life suddenly and becomes businesslike.)*

Harry: Now, for the haircut! *(He removes the towel he had wrapped around the* WRITER'S *head.)*
The writer: Take your time.
Harry: *(He examines the shears, clippers, and combs.)* Let's see now.

(The WRITER *turns and watches. A gasoline station* ATTENDANT *comes to the door.)*

The attendant *(to the* WRITER): Just wanted to say your car's ready now.
The writer: Thanks.

(The ATTENDANT *goes out.)*

The writer: Look. I'll tell you what. How much is a haircut?
Harry: Well, the regular price is a dollar. It's too much for a haircut, though, so I generally take a half or a quarter.
The writer *(getting out of the chair):* I've changed my mind. I don't want a haircut after all, but here's a dollar just the same. *(He hands* HARRY *a dollar, and he himself removes the apron.)*
Harry: It won't take a minute.
The writer: I know.
Harry: You don't have to pay me a dollar for a hot towel. My compliments.
The writer: That's O.K. *(He goes to the door.)*
Harry: Well, take it easy now.

The writer: Thanks. *(He stands a moment, thinking, then turns.)* Do you mind if I have a look at that oyster?

Harry: Not at all.

(The WRITER *goes to the shelf where* HARRY *has placed the oyster, picks it up, looks at it thoughtfully, puts it back without comment, but instead of leaving the shop, he looks around at the stuff in it. He then sits down on a wicker chair in the corner and lights a cigarette.)*

The writer: You know, they've got a gadget in New York now like a safety razor that anybody can give anybody else a haircut with.

Harry: They have?

The writer: Yeah, there was a full-page ad about it in last Sunday's *Times.*

Harry: Is that where you were last Sunday?

The writer: Yeah.

Harry: You been doing a lot of driving.

The writer: I like to drive. I don't know, though—those gadgets don't always work. They're asking two-ninety-five for it. You take a big family. The father could save a lot of money giving his kids a haircut.

Harry: Sounds like a great idea.

The writer: Question of effectiveness. If the father gives the boy a haircut the boy's ashamed of, well, that's not so good.

Harry: No, a boy likes to get a professional-looking haircut all right.

The writer: I thought I'd buy one, but I don't know.

Harry: You got a big family?

The writer: I mean for myself. But I don't know—there's something to be said for going to a barber shop once in a while. No use putting the barbers out of business.

Harry: Sounds like a pretty good article, though.

The writer *(getting up lazily):* Well, it's been nice talking to you.

(WOZZECK, *carrying a satchel, comes in, followed by* CLAY, ROXANNA, *and* GREELEY.)

Wozzeck: What's this all about, Harry?

Harry: I've got an oyster I want you to open.

Wozzeck: That's what the kids have been telling me.

Roxanna: *He* doesn't believe there's a pearl in the oyster, either.

Wozzeck: Of course not! What foolishness!

Clay: There's a *big* pearl in it.

Wozzeck: O.K., give me the oyster. I'll open it. Expert watch repairer, to open an oyster!

Harry: How much is a big pearl worth, Louie?

Wozzeck: Oh, a hundred. Two hundred, maybe.

Harry: A very big one?

Wozzeck: Three, maybe.

The writer: I've looked at that oyster, and I'd like to buy it. *(To* CLAY.) How much do you want for it?

Clay: I don't know.

The writer: How about three hundred?

Greeley: Three hundred dollars?

Clay: Is it all right, Mr. Van Dusen?

Harry: *(He looks at the* WRITER, *who nods.)* Sure it's all right.

(The WRITER *hands* CLAY *the money.)*

Clay *(looking at the money and then at the* WRITER): But suppose there ain't a pearl in it?

The writer: There *is,* though.

Wozzeck: Don't you want to open it first?

The writer: No, I want the whole thing. I don't think the pearl's stopped growing.

Clay: He says there *is* a pearl in the oyster, Mr. Van Dusen.

Harry: I think there is, too, Clay; so why don't you just go on home and give the money to your mother?

Clay: Well . . . I *knew* I was going to find something good today!

(The children go out. WOZZECK *is bewildered.)*

Wozzeck: Three hundred dollars! How do you know there's a pearl in it?

The writer: As far as I'm concerned, the whole thing's a pearl.

Wozzeck *(a little confused):* Well, I got to get back to the shop, Harry.

Harry: Thanks for coming by.

(WOZZECK *goes out. The* WRITER *holds the oyster in front of him as if it were an egg and looks at it carefully, turning it in his fingers. As he is doing so,* CLARK LARRABEE *comes into the shop. He is holding the copy of the newspaper that* HARRY *gave him.)*

Clark: We were ten miles up the highway when I happened to see this classified ad in the paper. *(He hands the paper to* HARRY *and sits down in the chair.)* I'm going out to the house, after all. Just for the weekend, of course, then back to work in Salinas again. Two or three months, I think I'll have enough to come back for a long time. Clay come by?

Harry: No. I've got the money here.

Clark: O.K., I'll take it out myself, but first let me have the works—shave, haircut, shampoo, massage.

Harry *(putting an apron on* CLARK): Sure thing, Clark. *(He bends the chair back and begins to lather* CLARK'S *face.)*

(MISS McCUTCHEON, *dressed neatly, looking like another person almost, comes in.)*

Miss McCutcheon: Well?

Harry: You look fine, Miss McCutcheon.

Miss McCutcheon: I don't mean that. I mean the oyster.

Harry: Oh, that! There *was* a pearl in it.

Miss McCutcheon: I don't believe it.

Harry: A *big* pearl.

Miss McCutcheon: You might have done me the courtesy of waiting until I had come back before opening it.

Harry: Couldn't wait.

Miss McCutcheon: Well, I don't believe you, but I've come for my haircut. I'll sit down and wait my turn.

Harry: Mr. Larrabee wants the works. You'll have to wait a long time.

Miss McCutcheon: Mr. Larrabee? Clay's father? Roxanna's father?

(CLARK *sits up.)*

Harry: Clark, I'd like you to meet our new teacher, Miss McCutcheon.

Clark: How do you do.

Miss McCutcheon: How do you do, Mr. Larrabee. *(She looks bewildered.)* Well, perhaps some other time, then, Mr. Van Dusen.

(She goes out. CLARK *sits back.* JUDGE APPLEGARTH *stops at the doorway of the shop.)*

The Judge: Not one thing on the beach, Harry. Not a blessed thing worth picking up and taking home.

(JUDGE APPLEGARTH *goes on. The* WRITER *looks at* HARRY.)

Harry: See what I mean?

The writer: Yeah. Well . . . so long. *(He puts the oyster in his coat pocket.)*

Harry: Drop in again any time you're driving to Hollywood.

The writer: Or away.

(He goes out.)

Clark *(after a moment):* You know, Harry, that boy of mine, Clay . . . well, a fellow like that, you can't just go off and leave him.

Harry: Of course you can't, Clark.

Clark: I'm taking him fishing tomorrow morning. How about going along, Harry?

Harry: Sure, Clark. Be like old times again. *(There is a pause.)*

Clark: What's all this about an oyster and a pearl?

Harry: Oh, just having a little fun with the new teacher. You know, she came in here and asked me to give her a poodle haircut? A poodle haircut! I don't believe I remember what a poodle *dog* looks like, even.

Why do you suppose the writer says "the whole thing's a pearl"?

Is this incident an example of "A Helping Hand"?

Do you agree with Miss McCutcheon that facing reality is the important thing? Or do you agree with Harry that reality can wait?

Ha'Penny

Alan Paton

Of the six hundred boys at the reformatory, about one hundred were from ten to fourteen years of age. My Department had from time to time expressed the intention of taking them away, and of establishing a special institution for them, more like an industrial school than a reformatory. This would have been a good thing, for their offences were very trivial, and they would have been better by themselves. Had such a school been established, I should have liked to have been Principal of it myself, for it would have been an easier job; small boys turn instinctively towards affection, and one controls them by it, naturally and easily.

Some of them, if I came near them, either on parade or in school or at football, would observe me watchfully, not directly or fully, but obliquely and secretly; sometimes I would surprise them at it, and make some small sign of recognition, which would satisfy them so that they would cease to observe me, and would give their full attention to the event of the moment. But I knew that my authority was thus confirmed and strengthened.

These secret relations with them were a source of continuous pleasure to me. Had they been my own children I would no doubt have given a greater expression to it. But often I would move through the silent and orderly parade, and stand by one of them. He would look straight in front of him with a little frown of concentration that expressed both childish awareness of and manly indifference to my nearness. Sometimes I would tweak his ear, and he would give me a brief smile of acknowledgment, or frown with still greater concentration. It was natural I suppose to confine these outward expressions to the very smallest, but they were taken as symbolic, and some older boys would observe them and take themselves to be included. It was a relief, when the reformatory was passing through times of turbulence and trouble, and when there was danger of estrangement between authority and boys, to make these simple and natural gestures, which were reassurances both to me and them that nothing important had changed.

On Sunday afternoons when I was on duty, I would take my car to the reformatory and watch the free boys being signed out at the gate. This simple operation was also watched by many boys not free, who would tell each other "in so many weeks I'll be signed out myself." Amongst the watchers were always some of the small boys, and these I would take by turns in the car. We would go out to the Potchefstroom Road with its ceaseless stream of traffic, and to the Baragwanath crossroads, and come back by the Van Wyksrus road to the reformatory. I would talk to them about their families, their parents, their sisters and brothers, and I would pretend to know nothing of Durban, Port Elizabeth,

Potchefstroom, and Clocolan, and ask them if these places were bigger than Johannesburg.

One of the small boys was Ha'penny, and he was about twelve years old. He came from Bloemfontein and was the biggest talker of them all. His mother worked in a white person's house, and he had two brothers and two sisters. His brothers were Richard and Dickie and his sisters Anna and Mina.

"Richard and Dickie?" I asked.

"Yes, *meneer.*"

"In English," I said, "Richard and Dickie are the same name."

When we returned to the reformatory, I sent for Ha'penny's papers; there it was plainly set down, Ha'penny was a waif, with no relatives at all. He had been taken in from one home to another, but he was naughty and uncontrollable, and eventually had taken to pilfering at the market.

I then sent for the Letter Book, and found that Ha'penny wrote regularly, or rather that others wrote for him till he could write himself, to Mrs. Betty Maarman, of 48 Vlak Street, Bloemfontein. But Mrs. Maarman had never once replied to him. When questioned, he had said, perhaps she is sick. I sat down and wrote at once to the Social Welfare Officer at Bloemfontein, asking him to investigate.

The next time I had Ha'penny out in the car, I questioned him again about his family. And he told me the same as before, his mother, Richard and Dickie, Anna and Mina. But he softened the "D" of "Dickie," so that it sounded now like Tickie.

"I thought you said Dickie," I said.

"I said Tickie," he said.

He watched me with concealed apprehension, and I came to the conclusion that this waif of Bloemfontein was a clever boy, who had told me a story that was all imagination, and had changed one single letter of it to make it safe from any question. And I thought I understood it all too, that he was ashamed of being without a family, and had invented them all, so that no one might discover that he was fatherless and motherless, and that no one in the world cared whether he was alive or dead. This gave me a strong feeling for him, and I went out of my way to manifest towards him that fatherly care that the State, though not in those words, had enjoined upon me by giving me this job.

Then the letter came from the Social Welfare Officer in Bloemfontein, saying that Mrs. Betty Maarman of 48 Vlak Street was a real person, and that she had four children, Richard and Dickie, Anna and Mina, but that Ha'penny was no child of hers, and she knew him only as a derelict of the streets. She had never answered his letters, because he wrote to her as *mother,* and she was no mother of his, nor did she wish to play any such role. She was a decent woman, a faithful member of the church, and she had no thought of corrupting her family by letting them have anything to do with such a child.

But Ha'penny seemed to me anything but the usual delinquent: his desire to have a family was so strong, and his reformatory record was so blameless, and his anxiety to please and obey so great, that I began to feel a great duty towards him. Therefore I asked him about his "mother."

He could not speak enough of her, nor with too high praise. She was loving, honest, and strict. Her home was clean. She had affection for all her children. It was clear that the homeless child, even as he had attached himself to me, would have attached himself to her; he had observed her even as he had observed me, but did not know the secret of how to open her heart, so that she would take him in, and save him from the lonely life that he led.

"Why did you steal when you had such a mother?" I asked.

He could not answer that; not all his brains nor his courage could find an answer to such a question, for he knew that with such a mother he would not have stolen at all.

"The boy's name is Dickie," I said, "not Tickie."

And then he knew the deception was revealed. Another boy might have said, "I told you it was Dickie," but he was too intelligent for that; he knew that if I had established that the boy's name was *Dickie,* I must have established other things too. I was shocked by the immediate and visible effect of my action. His whole brave assurance died within him, and he stood there exposed, not as a liar, but as a homeless child who had surrounded himself with mother, brothers, and sisters who did not exist. I had shattered the very foundations of his pride, and his sense of human significance.

He fell sick at once, and the doctor said it was tuberculosis. I wrote at once to Mrs. Maarman, telling her the whole story, of how this small boy had observed her, and had decided that she was the person he desired for his mother. But she wrote back saying that she could take no responsibility for him. For one thing, Ha'penny was a Mosuto, and she was a coloured woman; for another, she had never had a child in trouble, and how could she take such a boy?

Tuberculosis is a strange thing; sometimes it manifests itself suddenly in the most unlikely host, and swiftly sweeps to the end. Ha'penny withdrew himself from the world, from all Principals and mothers, and the doctor said there was little hope. In desperation I sent money for Mrs. Maarman to come.

She was a decent homely woman, and seeing that the situation was serious, she, without fuss or embarrassment, adopted Ha'penny for her own. The whole reformatory accepted her as his mother. She sat the whole day with him, and talked to him of Richard and Dickie, Anna and Mina, and how they were all waiting for him to come home. She poured out her affection on him, and had no fear of his sickness, nor did she allow it to prevent her from satisfying his hunger to be owned. She talked to him of what they would do when he came back, and how he would go to the school, and what they would buy for Guy Fawkes night.

He in his turn gave his whole attention to her, and when I visited him he was grateful, but I had passed out of his world. I felt judged in that I had sensed only the existence and not the measure of his desire. I wished I had done something sooner, more wise, more prodigal.

We buried him on the reformatory farm, and Mrs. Maarman said to me, "when you put up the cross, put he was my son."

"I'm ashamed," she said, "that I wouldn't take him."

"The sickness," I said, "the sickness would have come."

"No," she said, shaking her head with certainty. "It wouldn't have come. And if it had come at home, it would have been different."

So she left for Bloemfontein, after her strange visit to a reformatory. And I was left too, with the resolve to be more prodigal in the task that the State, though not in so many words, had enjoined on me.

The Gift of the Magi

O. Henry

One dollar and eighty-seven cents. That was all. And sixty cents of it was in pennies. Pennies saved one and two at a time by bulldozing the grocer and the vegetable man and the butcher until one's cheeks burned with the silent imputation of parsimony that such close dealing implied. Three times Della counted it. One dollar and eighty-seven cents. And the next day would be Christmas.

There was clearly nothing to do but flop down on the shabby little couch and howl. So Della did it. Which instigates the moral reflection that life is made up of sobs, sniffles, and smiles, with sniffles predominating.

While the mistress of the home is gradually subsiding from the first stage to the second, take a look at the home. A furnished flat at $8 per week. It did not exactly beggar description, but it certainly had that word on the lookout for the mendicancy squad.

In the vestibule below was a letter-box into which no letter would go, and an electric button from which no mortal finger could coax a ring. Also appertaining thereunto was a card bearing the name "Mr. James Dillingham Young."

The "Dillingham" had been flung to the breeze during a former period of prosperity when its possessor was being paid $30 per week. Now, when the income was shrunk to $20, the letters of "Dillingham" looked blurred, as though they were thinking seriously of contracting to a modest and unassuming D. But whenever Mr. James Dillingham Young came home and reached his flat above he was called "Jim" and greatly hugged by Mrs. James Dillingham Young, already introduced to you as Della. Which is all very good.

Della finished her cry and attended to her cheeks with the powder rag. She stood by the window and looked out dully at a gray cat walking a gray fence in a gray backyard. Tomorrow would be Christmas Day, and she had only $1.87 with which to buy Jim a present. She had been saving every penny she could for months, with this result. Twenty dollars a week doesn't go far. Expenses had been greater than she had calculated. They always are. Only $1.87 to buy a present for Jim. Her Jim. Many a happy hour she had spent planning for something nice for him. Something fine and rare and sterling–something just a little bit near to being worthy of the honor of being owned by Jim.

There was a pier-glass between the windows of the room. Perhaps you have seen a pier-glass in an $8 flat. A very thin and very agile person may, by observing his reflection in a rapid sequence of longitudinal strips, obtain a fairly accurate conception of his looks. Della, being slender, had mastered the art.

Suddenly she whirled from the window and stood before the glass. Her eyes were shining brilliantly, but her face had lost its color within twenty seconds. Rapidly she pulled down her hair and let it fall to its full length.

Now, there were two possessions of the James Dillingham Youngs in which they both took a mighty pride. One was Jim's gold watch that had been his father's and his grandfather's. The other was Della's hair. Had the Queen of Sheba lived in the flat across the airshaft, Della would have let her hair hang out the window some day to dry just to depreciate Her Majesty's jewels and gifts. Had King Solomon been the janitor, with all his treasures piled up in the basement, Jim would have pulled out his watch every time he passed, just to see him pluck at his beard from envy.

So now Della's beautiful hair fell about her rippling and shining like a cascade of brown waters. It reached below her knee and made itself almost a garment for her. And then she did it up again nervously and quickly. Once she faltered for a minute and stood still while a tear or two splashed on the worn red carpet.

On went her old brown jacket; on went her old brown hat. With a whirl of skirts and with the brilliant sparkle still in her eyes, she fluttered out the door and down the stairs to the street.

Where she stopped the sign read: "Mme. Sofronie. Hair Goods of All Kinds." One flight up Della ran, and collected herself, panting. Madame, large, too white, chilly, hardly looked the "Sofronie."

"Will you buy my hair?" asked Della.

"I buy hair," said Madame. "Take yer hat off and let's have a sight at the looks of it."

Down rippled the brown cascade.

"Twenty dollars," said Madame, lifting the mass with a practised hand.

"Give it to me quick," said Della.

Oh, and the next two hours tripped by on rosy wings. Forget the hashed metaphor. She was ransacking the stores for Jim's present.

She found it at last. It surely had been made for Jim and no one else. There was no other like it in any of the stores, and she had turned all of them inside out. It was a platinum fob chain simple and chaste in design, properly proclaiming its value by substance alone and not by meretricious ornamentation—as all good things should do. It was even worthy of The Watch. As soon as she saw it she knew that it must be Jim's. It was like him. Quietness and value—the description applied to both. Twenty-one dollars they took from her for it, and she hurried home with the 87 cents. With that chain on his watch Jim might be properly anxious about the time in any company. Grand as the watch was, he sometimes looked at it on the sly on account of the old leather strap that he used in place of a chain.

When Della reached home her intoxication gave way a little to prudence and reason. She got out her curling irons and lighted the gas and went to work repairing the ravages made by generosity added to love. Which is always a tremendous task, dear friends—a mammoth task.

Within forty minutes her head was covered with tiny, close-lying curls that made her look wonderfully like a truant schoolboy. She looked at her reflection in the mirror long, carefully, and critically.

"If Jim doesn't kill me," she said to herself, "before he takes a second look at me, he'll say I look like a Coney Island chorus girl. But what could I do—oh! what could I do with a dollar and eighty-seven cents?"

At 7 o'clock the coffee was made and the frying-pan was on the back of the stove hot and ready to cook the chops.

Jim was never late. Della doubled the fob chain in her hand and sat on the corner of the table near the door that he always entered. Then she heard his step on the stair way down on the first flight, and she turned white for just a moment. She had a habit of saying little silent prayers about the simplest everyday things, and now she whispered: "Please God, make him think I am still pretty."

The door opened and Jim stepped in and closed it. He looked thin and very serious. Poor fellow, he was only twenty-two—and to be burdened with a family! He needed a new overcoat and he was without gloves.

Jim stopped inside the door, as immovable as a setter at the scent of quail. His eyes were fixed upon Della, and there was an expression in them that she could not read, and it terrified her. It was not anger, nor surprise, nor disapproval, nor horror, nor any of the sentiments that she had been prepared for. He simply stared at her fixedly with that peculiar expression on his face.

Della wriggled off the table and went for him.

"Jim, darling," she cried, "don't look at me that way. I had my hair cut off and sold it because I couldn't have lived through Christmas without giving you a present. It'll grow out again—you won't mind, will you? I just had to do it. My hair grows awfully fast. Say 'Merry Christmas!' Jim, and let's be happy. You don't know what a nice—what a beautiful, nice gift I've got for you."

"You've cut off your hair?" asked Jim, laboriously, as if he had not arrived at that patent fact yet even after the hardest mental labor.

"Cut it off and sold it," said Della. "Don't you like me just as well, anyhow? I'm me without my hair, ain't I?"

Jim looked about the room curiously.

"You say your hair is gone?" he said, with an air almost of idiocy.

"You needn't look for it," said Della. "It's sold, I tell you—sold and gone, too. It's Christmas Eve, boy. Be good to me, for it went for you. Maybe the hairs of my head were numbered," she went on with a sudden serious sweetness, "but nobody could ever count my love for you. Shall I put the chops on, Jim?"

Out of his trance Jim seemed quickly to wake. He enfolded his Della. For ten seconds let us regard with discreet scrutiny some inconsequential object in the other direction. Eight dollars a week or a million a year—what is the difference? A mathematician or a wit would give you the wrong answer. The magi brought valuable gifts, but that was not among them. This dark assertion will be illuminated later on.

Jim drew a package from his overcoat pocket and threw it upon the table.

"Don't make any mistake, Dell," he said, "about me. I don't think there's anything in the way of a haircut or a shave or a shampoo that could make me like my girl any less. But if you'll unwrap that package you may see why you had me going a while at first."

White fingers and nimble tore at the string and paper. And then an ecstatic scream of joy; and then, alas! a quick feminine change to hysterical tears and wails, necessitating the immediate employment of all the comforting powers of the lord of the flat.

For there lay The Combs—the set of combs, side and back, that Della had worshipped for long in a Broadway window. Beautiful combs, pure tortoise shell, with jewelled rims—just the shade to wear in the beautiful vanished hair. They were expensive combs, she knew, and her heart had simply craved and yearned over them without the least hope of possession. And now, they were hers, but the tresses that should have adorned the coveted adornments were gone.

But she hugged them to her bosom, and at length she was able to look up with dim eyes and a smile and say: "My hair grows so fast, Jim!"

And then Della leaped up like a little singed cat and cried, "Oh, oh!"

Jim had not yet seen his beautiful present. She held it out to him eagerly upon her open palm. The dull precious metal seemed to flash with a reflection of her bright and ardent spirit.

"Isn't it a dandy, Jim? I hunted all over town to find it. You'll have to look at the time a hundred times a day now. Give me your watch. I want to see how it looks on it."

Instead of obeying, Jim tumbled down on the couch and put his hands under the back of his head and smiled.

"Dell," said he, "let's put our Christmas presents away and keep 'em a while. They're too nice to use just at present. I sold the watch to get the money to buy your combs. And now suppose you put the chops on."

The magi, as you know, were wise men—wonderfully wise men—who brought gifts to the Babe in the manger. They invented the art of giving Christmas presents. Being wise, their gifts were no doubt wise ones, possibly bearing the privilege of exchange in case of duplication. And here I have lamely related to you the uneventful chronicle of two foolish children in a flat who most unwisely sacrificed for each other the greatest treasures of their house. But in a last word to the wise of these days let it be said that of all who give gifts these two were the wisest. Of all who give and receive gifts, such as they are wisest. Everywhere they are wisest. They are the magi.

In the last paragraph of the story, when O. Henry refers to "two foolish children in a flat who most unwisely sacrificed for each other the greatest treasures of their house," does he really mean "foolish" and "most unwisely"? If the author were attempting to express his feelings directly, what other words might he have used?

How would you define "love" if you had only this story from which to form your definition?

This Thing Called Love Is Pathological

Lawrence Casler

[1] Magazines, movies, and television teach us the joys of love. Advertisers insist that we must look good and smell good in order to escape being lonely and loveless. Artists, philosophers, and hippies try to convince us of their different ideas of what love is; and most psychotherapists say that the ability to love is a sign—sometimes *the* sign—of mental health.

[2] To suggest that the importance of love is overemphasized is to risk being accused of coldness, low self-image, or some kind of sickness. Still, the expanding frontiers of psychology require a reconsideration of love at this time.

[3] We shall be concerned, chiefly, with what is generally called "romantic" love. Love, like other emotions, has causes, characteristics, and consequences. Temporarily setting aside the question of why, or whether, love makes the world go 'round, makes life worth living, and conquers all, let's consider the somewhat easier question of what causes people to fall in love.

[4] Most individuals in our society feel insecure; because of this insecurity they need to find people who accept and agree with their ideas, and approve of their actions. Part of this need is inescapable. Life requires continual decision-making: a red vs. a green tie, honesty vs. dishonesty, etc. When we are unsure of ourselves, we need to know that we are making the right decisions. We are, therefore, delighted when we meet someone who likes the same kind of dance music or peanut butter that we like. If we find a person whose choices in many different matters are the same as our own, we will value this person because he supports and builds up our opin-

ion of ourself. This attachment to someone who agrees with us constitutes one important basis for love.

[5] While the relationship between loving and being loved is very close, love is not automatically reciprocated. Indeed, it may lead to feelings of dislike if the individual's self-image is already low: "Anyone who says he loves *me* must be kidding—or a fool." Still, a person is relatively likely to love someone who loves him.

[6] A young woman, for any of several reasons, may *pretend* to like her date more than she really cares for him. The man, hungry for affection, responds in the same way. Then the woman, pleased because the man seems to like her, feels the fondness she had once pretended. Falling in love may be regarded, in cases such as these, as a snowball with a hollow core.

[7] Nevertheless, we do not fall in love with everyone who accepts us. Other needs clamor for satisfaction. And the more needs that one person satisfies, the more likely we are to love that person. One of the strongest needs is called, very loosely, sex. We love someone not simply because he boosts our ego, but because he is an ego-booster with sex appeal.

[8] For most of us, the pressures to fall in love are so great that we can no longer "choose" to love or not love. Loving becomes inevitable, like dying or getting married. We are so thoroughly brainwashed that we come to pity or scorn the person who is not in love. (Of course, we may feel pity or scorn for ourselves, but not for long: anyone who does not have the inner resources to stand alone can usually find a person who also needs someone to lean on.)

[9] Our society, besides being love-oriented, is marriage-oriented. From early childhood on, we hear countless statements beginning: "when (not *if*) you get married. . . ." And, just as love is regarded as a prerequisite

for sex, love is also considered a prerequisite for marriage. Consequently, the insecurity and the fear of social punishment that force many of us into marriage provide additional powerful motives for falling in love.

[10] Let us turn now to a consideration of the *consequences* of love. First, being in love makes it easier to view oneself as a normal, healthy citizen of the Western world. Love also tends to change certain psychological processes. There is a saying: "A woman is beautiful only when she is loved." The statement, however, is not quite accurate. A woman (likewise a man, a worm, a grain of sand) may become beautiful when the person looking at her has been given LSD or anything else that can induce hallucinations. In short, love may create the error of overevaluation. The doting lover is doomed either to painful disillusion or to the permanent delusion that so closely resembles psychosis.

[11] Some may argue that I am speaking of immature infatuation rather than real love. Mature love, they may insist, is a broadening, deepening experience. The claim that love promotes maturity is not convincing unless it can be proved that the individual would not have matured if he had not fallen in love. Indeed, to the extent that love fosters dependency, it may be viewed as a deterrent to maturity.

[12] I am not asserting that the effects of love always border on the pathological. I am saying that the person who seeks love in order to obtain security will become, like an alcoholic, increasingly dependent on this source of illusory well-being. The secure person who seeks love would probably not trap himself in this way.

[13] If the need for a love relationship is based largely on insecurity and conformity to social pressure, then the person who is secure and independent will not need

to love. He will, rather, be a person who does not find his own company boring—a person whose inner resources are such that other persons, although they provide pleasure and stimulation, are not absolutely necessary. For a long time, we have been told to love others as we love ourselves. But perhaps we seek love relationships with others only because we do not love ourselves enough.

[14] What would a healthy, love-free person be like? One might assume that coldness would be among his characteristics. But a cold person is simply one who does not give us the warmth we want or need. Describing someone as cold says more about the person who is doing the describing than it does about the person being described. Absence of warmth is responded to negatively only by insecure persons who interpret it as rejection.

[15] Would the love-free person be egotistical? Perhaps, but only if that term is relieved of its ugly connotations. To be self-centered does not mean to disregard the worth of other people. It does imply that other people are reacted to within a frame of reference that is centered on the self. There is nothing bad about this. In fact, psychologists would probably accept the position that we are all self-centered. No matter how other-directed our actions may appear, they are functions of *our* perception of the world, based, in turn, on *our* previous experiences. Since every act is a "self-ish" one, we should only judge the *effects* of selfishness, rather than condemn selfishness itself.

[16] This essay has not been anti-love, but pro-people. I view society's emphasis on love as both an effect and a cause of the insecurity, dependency, and frightened conformity that may be the death of us all. To love a person means, all too often, to use that person. And exploitation, even if mutual, is incompatible with

human growth. Finally, like a crutch, love may keep us from exercising our own potential for growth.

[17] Perhaps the goal of social reformers should be not love, but respect—for others, and most of all, for self.

The author says, "To love a person means, all too often, to use that person." Do you agree with that? In what sense is it possible to "use" people while appearing to love them?

The Practice of Love

Erich Fromm

What does it mean to "love one another"? To get a grasp on the answer offered by this writer, read the first two paragraphs and then just the first sentence of the other paragraphs until you get to the end. Read the last two paragraphs in their entirety too and ask yourself what he's told you about love. If you're uncertain about some things, go back and read more of the paragraph until you're sure you've got it.

Faith is an indispensable quality of any significant friendship or love. "Having faith" in another person means to be certain of the reliability and unchangeability of his fundamental attitudes, of the core of his personality, of his love. By this I do not mean that a person may not change his opinions, but that his basic motivations remain the same; that, for instance, his respect for life and human dignity is part of himself, not subject to change.

In the same sense we have faith in ourselves. We are aware of the existence of a self, of a core in our personality which is unchangeable and which persists throughout our life in spite of varying circumstances, and regardless of certain changes in opinions and feelings. It is this core which is the reality behind the word "I," and on which our conviction of our own identity is based. Unless we have faith in the persistence of our self, our feeling of identity is threatened, and we become dependent on other people whose approval then becomes the basis for our feeling of identity.

Only the person who has faith in himself is able to be faithful to others, because only he can be sure that he will be the same at a future time as he is today, and, therefore, that he will feel and act as he now expects to. Faith in oneself is a condition of our ability to promise, and since, as Nietzsche said, man can be defined by his capacity to promise, faith is one of the conditions of human existence. What matters in relation to love is the faith in one's own love; in its ability to produce love in others, and in its reliability.

To have faith requires *courage,* the ability to take a risk, the readiness even to accept pain and disappointment. Whoever insists on safety and security as primary conditions of life cannot have faith; whoever shuts himself off in a system of defense, where distance and possession are his means of security, makes himself a prisoner. To be loved, and to love, need courage, the courage to judge certain values as of ultimate concern—and to take the jump and stake everything on these values.

This courage is very different from the courage of which that famous braggart Mussolini spoke when he used the slogan "to live dangerously." His kind of courage is the courage of nihilism. It is rooted in a destructive attitude toward life, in the willingness to throw away life because one is incapable of loving it. The courage of despair is the opposite of the courage of love, just as the faith in power is the opposite of the faith in life.

Is there anything to be practiced about faith and courage? Indeed, faith can be practiced at every moment. It takes faith to bring up a child; it takes faith to fall asleep; it takes faith to begin any work. But we all are accustomed to having this kind of faith. Whoever does not have it suffers from overanxiety about his child, or from insomnia, or from the inability to do any kind of productive work; or he is suspicious, restrained from being close to anybody, or hypochondriacal, or unable to make any long-range plans.

To stick to one's judgment about a person even if public opinion or some unforeseen facts seem to invalidate it, to stick to one's convictions even though they are unpopular—all this requires faith and courage. To take the difficulties, setbacks, and sorrows of life as a challenge which to overcome makes us stronger, rather than as unjust punishment which should not happen to *us,* requires faith and courage.

The practice of faith and courage begins with the small details of daily life. The first step is to notice where and when one loses faith, to look through the rationalizations which are used to cover up this loss of faith, to recognize where one acts in a cowardly way, and again how one rationalizes it. To recognize how every betrayal of faith weakens one, and how increased weakness leads to new betrayal, and so on, in a vicious circle. Then one will also recognize that *while one is consciously afraid of not being loved, the real, though usually unconscious, fear is that of loving.*

To love means to commit oneself without guarantee, to give oneself completely in the hope that our love will produce love in the loved person. Love is an act of faith, and whoever is of little faith is also of little love. Can one say more about the practice of faith? Someone else might; if I were a poet or a preacher, I might try. But since I am not either of these, I cannot even try to say more about the practice of faith, but am sure that anyone who is really concerned can learn to have faith as a child learns to walk.

One attitude, indispensable for the practice of the art of loving, which thus far has been mentioned only implicitly should be discussed explicitly since it is basic for the practice of love: *activity*. By activity is not meant "doing something," but an inner activity, the productive use of one's powers. Love is an activity; if I love, I am in a constant state of active concern with the loved person, but not only with him or her. For I shall become incapable of relating myself actively to the loved person if I am lazy, if I am not in a constant state of awareness, alertness, activity. Sleep is the only proper situation for inactivity; the state of awakeness is one in which laziness should have no place. The paradoxical situation with a vast number of people today is that they are half-asleep when awake, and half-awake when asleep, or when they want to sleep.

To be fully awake is the condition for not being bored, or being boring—and indeed, not to be bored or boring is one of the main conditions for loving. To be active in thought, feeling, with one's eyes and ears, throughout the day, to avoid inner laziness, be it in the form of being receptive, hoarding, or plain wasting one's time, is an indispensable condition for the practice of the art of loving. It is an illusion to believe that one can separate life in such a way that one is productive in the sphere of love and unproductive in all other spheres. Productiveness does not permit of such a division of labor. The capacity to love demands a state of intensity, awakeness, enhanced vitality, which can only be the result of a productive and active orientation in many other spheres of life. If one is not productive in other spheres, one is not productive in love either.

Why is faith so important in the practice of love? Why can't a lazy person be a loving person, according to the author?

The Greatest of These Is Love

(1 Corinthians 13)

1 If I had the gift of being able to speak in other
languages without learning them, and could speak in
every language there is in all of heaven and earth, but
didn't love others, I would only be making noise. 2 If I
had the gift of prophecy and knew all about what is
going to happen in the future, knew everything about
everything, but didn't love others, what good would it
do? Even if I had the gift of faith so that I could speak
to a mountain and make it move, I would still be worth
nothing at all without love. 3 If I gave everything I have
to poor people, and if I were burned alive for preaching
the Gospel but didn't love others, it would be of no
value whatever.

4 Love is very patient and kind, never jealous or
envious, never boastful or proud, 5 never haughty or
selfish or rude. Love does not demand its own way. It is
not irritable or touchy. It does not hold grudges and will
hardly even notice when others do it wrong. 6 It is never
glad about injustice, but rejoices whenever truth wins
out. 7 If you love someone you will be loyal to him no

matter what the cost. You will always believe in him,
always expect the best of him, and always stand your
ground in defending him.

8 All the special gifts and powers from God will someday come to an end, but love goes on forever. Someday
prophecy, and speaking in unknown languages, and special knowledge—these gifts will disappear. 9 Now we
know so little, even with our special gifts, and the
preaching of those most gifted is still so poor. 10 But
when we have been made perfect and complete, then
the need for these inadequate special gifts will come to
an end, and they will disappear.

11 It's like this: when I was a child I spoke and
thought and reasoned as a child does. But when I
became a man my thoughts grew far beyond those of
my childhood, and now I have put away the childish
things. 12 In the same way, we can see and understand
only a little about God now, as if we were peering at his
reflection in a poor mirror; but someday we are going to
see him in his completeness, face to face. Now all that I
know is hazy and blurred, but then I will see everything
clearly, just as clearly as God sees into my heart right
now.

13 There are three things that remain—faith, hope,
and love—and the greatest of these is love.

The Living Bible

The Prodigal Son

Young man—
Young man—
Your arm's too short to box with God.

But Jesus spake in a parable, and he said:
A certain man had two sons.
Jesus didn't give this man a name,
But his name is God Almighty.
And Jesus didn't call these sons by name,
But ev'ry young man,
Ev'rywhere,
Is one of these two sons.

And the younger son said to his father,
He said: Father, divide up the property,
And give me my portion now.

And the father with tears in his eyes said: Son,
Don't leave your father's house.
But the boy was stubborn in his head,
And haughty in his heart,
And he took his share of his father's goods,
And went into a far-off country.

There comes a time,
There comes a time
When ev'ry young man looks out from his father's
  house,
Longing for that far-off country.

And the young man journeyed on his way,
And he said to himself as he travelled along:
This sure is an easy road,

Nothing like the rough furrows behind my father's
plow.

Young man—
Young man—
Smooth and easy is the road
That leads to hell and destruction.
Down grade all the way,
The further you travel, the faster you go.
No need to trudge and sweat and toil,
Just slip and slide and slip and slide
Till you bang up against hell's iron gate.

And the younger son kept travelling along,
Till at night-time he came to a city.
And the city was bright in the night-time like day,
The streets all crowded with people,
Brass bands and string bands a-playing,
And ev'rywhere the young man turned
There was singing and laughing and dancing.
And he stopped a passer-by and he said:
Tell me what city is this?
And the passer-by laughed and said: Don't you know?
This is Babylon, Babylon,
That great city of Babylon.
Come on, my friend, and go along with me.
And the young man joined the crowd.

Young man—
Young man—
You're never lonesome in Babylon.
You can always join a crowd in Babylon.
Young man—
Young man—
You can never be alone in Babylon,

Alone with your Jesus in Babylon.
You can never find a place, a lonesome place,
A lonesome place to go down on your knees,
And talk with your God, in Babylon.
You're always in a crowd in Babylon.

And the young man went with his new-found friend,
And bought himself some brand new clothes,
And he spent his days in the drinking dens,
Swallowing the fires of hell.
And he spent his nights in the gambling dens,
Throwing dice with the devil for his soul.
And he met up with the women of Babylon.
Oh, the women of Babylon!
Dressed in yellow and purple and scarlet,
Loaded with rings and earrings and bracelets,
Their lips like a honeycomb dripping with honey,
Perfumed and sweet-smelling like a jasmine flower;
And the jasmine smell of the Babylon women
Got in his nostrils and went to his head,
And he wasted his substance in riotous living,
In the evening, in the black and dark of night,
With the sweet-sinning women of Babylon.
And they stripped him of his money,
And they stripped him of his clothes,
And they left him broke and ragged
In the streets of Babylon.

Then the young man joined another crowd—
The beggars and lepers of Babylon.
And he went to feeding swine,
And he was hungrier than the hogs;
He got down on his belly in the mire and mud
And ate the husks with the hogs.
And not a hog was too low to turn up his nose
At the man in the mire of Babylon.

Then the young man came to himself—
He came to himself and said:
In my father's house are many mansions,
Ev'ry servant in his house has bread to eat,
Ev'ry servant in his house has a place to sleep;

I will arise and go to my father.
And his father saw him afar off,
And he ran up the road to meet him.
He put clean clothes upon his back,
And a golden chain around his neck,
He made a feast and killed the fatted calf,
And invited the neighbors in.

Oh-o-oh, sinner,
When you're mingling with the crowd in Babylon—
Drinking the wine of Babylon—
Running with the women of Babylon—
You forget about God, and you laugh at Death.
Today you've got the strength of a bull in your neck
And the strength of a bear in your arms,
But some o' these days, some o' these days,
You'll have a hand-to-hand struggle with bony Death,
And Death is bound to win.

Young man, come away from Babylon,
That hell-border city of Babylon.
Leave the dancing and gambling of Babylon,
The wine and whiskey of Babylon,
The hot-mouthed women of Babylon;
Fall down on your knees,
And say in your heart:
I will arise and go to my Father.

James Weldon Johnson

Where does the actual parable end? To whom is the rest of the poem addressed?

Who is the "young man" in the poem?

The Revolutionary

Do you
wince when you hear his name
made vanity?

What if you were not so safe
sheltered, circled by love
and convention?
What if
the world shouted at you?
Could you take the string
of hoarse words—glutton,
wino, devil, crazy
man, agitator, bastard,
nigger-lover, rebel,
and hang the grimy ornament
around your neck
and answer
love?

See the sharp stones poised
against your head! even
your dear friend
couples your name with curses
("By God! I know not God!")
the obscene affirmation

of infidelity
echoes, insistent,
from a henhouse roof.

Then—Slap! Spit! the whip,
the thorn. The gravel
grinds your fallen knees
under a whole world's weight
until
the hammering home of all
your innocence
stakes you, stranded,
halfway between hilltop and heaven
(neither will have you).

And will you whisper
forgive?

Luci Shaw

Perfect Love Banishes Fear

1 John 4:18 (NEB)

The risk of love
is that of being unreturned.

For if I love too deep,
too hard, too long
and you love little
or you love
me not at all
then is my treasure given,
gone,
flown away lonely.

But if you give me back
passion for passion,
return my burning,
add your own
dark fire to flame my heart
then is love perfect
hot, round, augmented,
whole, endless, infinite,
and it is fear
that flies.

Luci Shaw

All Are Needed by Each One

(1 Corinthians 12)

1 And now, brothers, I want to write about the special
abilities the Holy Spirit gives to each of you, for I don't
want any misunderstanding about them. 2 You will remember that before you became Christians you went
around from one idol to another, not one of which
could speak a single word. 3 But now you are meeting
people who claim to speak messages from the Spirit of
God. How can you know whether they are really in-
spired by God or whether they are fakes? Here is the
test: no one speaking by the power of the Spirit of God
can curse Jesus, and no one can say, "Jesus is Lord,"
and really mean it, unless the Holy Spirit is helping him.

4 Now God gives us many kinds of special abilities,
but it is the same Holy Spirit who is the source of them
all. 5 There are different kinds of service to God, but it is
the same Lord we are serving. 6 There are many ways in
which God works in our lives, but it is the same God
who does the work in and through all of us who are his.
7 The Holy Spirit displays God's power through each of
us as a means of helping the entire church.

8 To one person the Spirit gives the ability to give
wise advice; someone else may be especially good at
studying and teaching, and this is his gift from the same
Spirit. 9 He gives special faith to another, and to someone else the power to heal the sick. 10 He gives power
for doing miracles to some, and to others power to
prophesy and preach. He gives someone else the power
to know whether evil spirits are speaking through those
who claim to be giving God's messages—or whether it is
really the Spirit of God who is speaking. Still another
person is able to speak in languages he never learned;
and others, who do not know the language either, are

given power to understand what he is saying. [11] It is the
same and only Holy Spirit who gives all these gifts and
powers, deciding which each one of us should have.

[12] Our bodies have many parts, but the many parts
make up only one body when they are all put together.
So it is with the "body" of Christ. [13] Each of us is a part
of the one body of Christ. Some of us are Jews, some
are Gentiles, some are slaves and some are free. But the
Holy Spirit has fitted us all together into one body. We
have been baptized into Christ's body by the one Spirit,
and have all been given that same Holy Spirit.

[14] Yes, the body has many parts, not just one part.
[15] If the foot says, "I am not a part of the body because
I am not a hand," that does not make it any less a part
of the body. [16] And what would you think if you heard
an ear say, "I am not part of the body because I am
only an ear, and not an eye"? Would that make it any
less a part of the body? [17] Suppose the whole body were
an eye—then how would you hear? Or if your whole
body were just one big ear, how could you smell anything?

[18] But that isn't the way God has made us. He has
made many parts for our bodies and has put each part
just where he wants it. [19] What a strange thing a body
would be if it had only one part! [20] So he has made
many parts, but still there is only one body.

[21] The eye can never say to the hand, "I don't need
you." The head can't say to the feet, "I don't need
you."

[22] And some of the parts that seem weakest and least
important are really the most necessary. [23] Yes, we are
especially glad to have some parts that seem rather odd!
And we carefully protect from the eyes of others those
parts that should not be seen, [24] while of course the
parts that may be seen do not require this special care.
So God has put the body together in such a way that

extra honor and care are given to those parts that might otherwise seem less important. [25] This makes for happiness among the parts, so that the parts have the same care for each other that they do for themselves. [26] If one part suffers, all parts suffer with it, and if one part is honored, all the parts are glad.

[27] Now here is what I am trying to say: All of you together are the one body of Christ and each one of you is a separate and necessary part of it. [28] Here is a list of

some of the parts he has placed in his church, which is his body:

Apostles,
Prophets—those who preach God's Word,
Teachers,
Those who do miracles,
Those who have the gift of healing,
Those who can help others,
Those who can get others to work together,
Those who speak in languages they have never learned.

29 Is everyone an apostle? Of course not. Is everyone a
preacher? No. Are all teachers? Does everyone have the
power to do miracles? 30 Can everyone heal the sick? Of
course not. Does God give all of us the ability to speak
in languages we've never learned? Can just anyone
understand and translate what those are saying who
have that gift of foreign speech? 31 No, but try your
best to have the more important of these gifts.

The Living Bible

Through the Midst of the Sea on Dry Ground

E. William Oldenburg

The church is Catholic, universal; so are all her actions: all that she does belongs to all. When she baptizes a child, that action concerns me, for that child is thereby connected to that Head which is my Head too, and engrafted into that body whereof I am a member.

—John Donne, *Meditation XVII*

a cloud moves, a shaft of sun
diffused and sprinkled
through stained glass
touches dipping fingers
and the wrinkled forehead
while it dazzles my eyes.
    into the name of the father
    and of the son
    and of the holy spirit. . . .
the parson's dipping fingers
flick quick
    the sleight of hand is faster than
    sun-struck eyes which
miss the ecclesiastical
slick trick
    this Sherri, Kim, or Debbie
    because of these few drops
    spittered on her pink forehead
has become a part of my future
whatever her own future
    gum-chewing cheerleader
    stewardess, spinster librarian
    feminist, fascist, adventuress,
    first lady, saint, or simpering
    society dame
all that she may do concerns me.

Who is the speaker in the poem? What does he believe? Do you agree? What are the implications?

Passion for Compassion

Keep open
to pain
his   hers   theirs
as well as yours

Threshold
deep   wide
for untranquilized
empathizers

Agony
can create capacity
to respond
in kind

Acute heartbreak
walks back
to gather pieces
bandage wounds

Sensitive
to all living
all suffering
let mercy thrive

Thomas John Carlisle

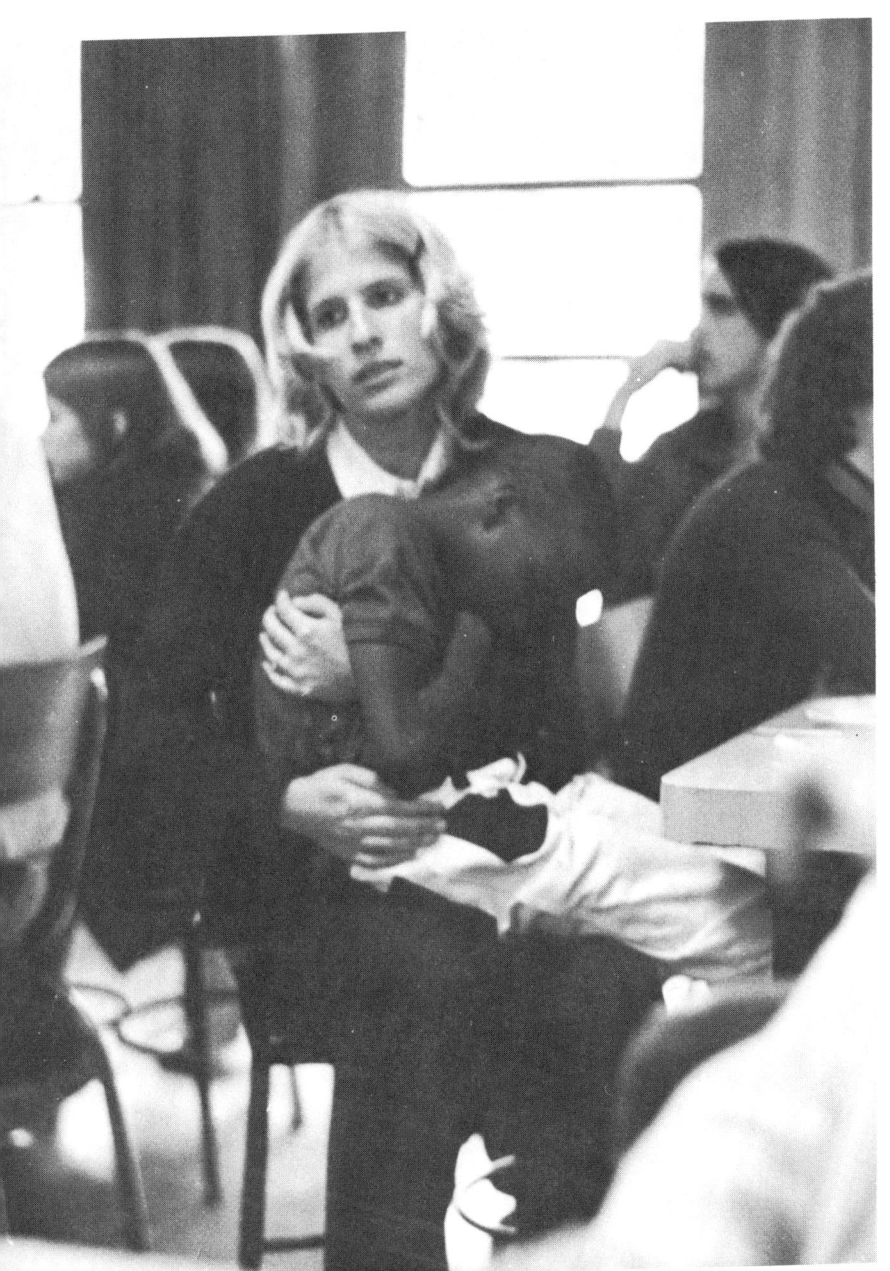

Safe at Sea

I prefer
magnificent distances
between me
and God.

Reserve me
a quiet cubicle
where my shipmates' screams
will be inaudible.

Let them wrestle
with revolutions.
I am resolved
to sleep soundly.

Thomas John Carlisle